Indian Heritage, Indian Pride

Indian Heritage, Indian Pride

Stories That Touched My Life

by Jimalee Burton
(Ho-chee-nee, Cherokee)

Foreword by W. W. Keeler
Principal Chief of the Cherokee Nation

Paintings and sketches by the author

University of Oklahoma Press : Norman

Publication of this book has been aided by a grant from the William G. Selby and Marie Selby Foundation, Sarasota, Florida

Library of Congress Cataloging in Publication Data

Burton, Jimalee.
Indian heritage, Indian pride. Stories that touched my life.
1. Indians of North America—Oklahoma. I. Title.
E78.045B93 970.4'66 73-7426
ISBN 0-8061-1124-0

 Composed and printed at Norman, Oklahoma, U.S.A., by the University of Oklahoma Press. First edition.

This book is dedicated to
my wonderful parents, James A. and Mary Chitwood
to my sister, Maudelia
and to all the great First Americans who built
Oklahoma—the Indians—and white friends

Foreword

"I hoped to give the Indian pride in his heritage," is what Jimalee Chitwood Burton says was a principal reason for writing this fine book. I cannot think of a better objective. In view of the shameful way Indians were treated for so long in America, and the distorted image so many people have had of Indians as no more than savages, American Indians—particularly young Indians—vitally need pride in themselves and their heritage. The book should accomplish this aim, for it accurately, and yet in colorful and often poetic language, tells the truth about the tremendous achievements of Indians from the earliest of times.

The book should also reveal to many white men that, contrary to the stereotyped image they have, the American Indian has a lot to be proud of—including great achievements in art, architecture, ecology, agriculture, and, most important, morality and the "art of living."

Mrs. Burton also tells the truth about special challenges American Indians face today to be truly free and what they must do to overcome them.

I have had the privilege of being acquainted with Mrs. Burton for many years and know that she is especially well qualified to write about her people. She came from a family that was active in the early development of the Southwest and grew up in Oklahoma. She herself is part Cherokee, and when she was a baby her father gave her the Cherokee name Ho-chee-nee, which, appropriately in her case, means "The Leader."

Mrs. Burton has an unusually sharp and inquisitive mind and at an early age began asking questions to try to understand what was going on around her. She has kept this up all her life. She has traveled widely to study native cultures and civilizations in many parts of the world. She is a talented artist and musician, as well as author and poet, and a warm-hearted person who is keenly interested in the people of her race. So Mrs. Burton has the background to write about the traditions, achievements, and challenges of her people which many who write about Indians do not have.

An example of Mrs. Burton's generosity is that she is donating all royalties from the sale of this book to the Cherokee Foundation, Bartlesville, Oklahoma, an organization which assists the Cherokee people in countless ways. I am sure that I speak for the Cherokee Nation generally in thanking her for this. We are also grateful to the Board of Directors of the William G. Selby and Marie Selby Foundation for making possible the publication of this book.

I personally am very happy that Mrs. Burton took on the difficult job of writing this book, for I know that it will do much to improve the understanding by others of American Indians, increase Indians' pride, and contribute to a better life for many Cherokees.

W. W. Keeler
Principal Chief
Cherokee Nation

Preface

This book had to materialize. After every program I give, my hearers ask, "Is this material in print? Where can I buy it?" Now this is it—a book of stories that have touched my life and those of my parents. At first hand I learned from my alert, discerning Cherokee parents the exhilarating and often tragic experiences lived by them, weaving these into my own life pattern as I grew up in the explosive days of Oklahoma and the real West.

At sixteen my father was a pony-express rider from Quitman to Quanah, Texas. In 1889 he was among the thundering thousands of stampeding, land-hungry people who swept into Indian Territory at a signal—the crack of a pistol, to take up homes in the new country. This was a terrific medley of humanity. Life was cheap, land the prize.

Indian Territory by sacred treaty belonged to the Indian. It was confiscated by the United States government, thrown open to settlement, a complete betrayal of a trust. These were thrilling days, terrible days for the helpless Indian silently watching. Though a daughter of both Indian and white cultures, I am always Indian, devoting my life to the cause of my people.

This book does not pretend to be an archaeological or ethnological report on the American Indian. I share with you, my reader, memories of a culture fast disappearing in the tide of assimilation. Soon it will be no more, remembered only in such stories as you will read here, while studying these paintings, of our brave, proud ancestors and their re-

Ho-Chee-Nee

ligious culture—superior in many ways to that of the invader. Their contribution to the world in foods, medicines, and fabulous architectural wonders confound the experts. Though their bones salt America from coast to coast, today there is but a remnant of a little-known people. Still they cling to their sacred religious beliefs, handed down through eons of time, their one sustaining foot to stand on. Many young Indians join the homogenizing tide. The old ones weep.

The American Indians have been the victims of one of the cruelest fates of history—corralled for a century, now struggling to free themselves, to join the business and cultural life of their country.

As a baby I was named Ho-chee-nee ("The Leader") by my father. Mother called me Jimalee. My early life revolved around their trading post in Oklahoma, where I acquired the stories and beliefs as told in this book. Daily I thank the Great Spirit for the many precious talents he so graciously loaned to me. I have recognized and used them faithfully.

My studies of native Indian culture have carried me far in the Western Hemisphere.—To Peru, to the high Andes, Panama, Guatemala, Mexico, the Virgin Islands, Canada, Alaska, and Hawaii. I traveled alone to meet, to know, and to join the native people for weeks at a time—to become one of them.

For fifteen years I was United States editor of *The Native Voice*, an all-Indian newspaper published in Vancouver, British Columbia.

My Indian stories, articles, and poems have appeared in many national publications. For ten years I wrote a radio poetry program for "Smiling Dan," broadcast over KTUL and KVOO, Tulsa, Oklahoma. My lectures on Indian tradition have been aired over the Voice of America, and educational television for schools and clubs.

I have a boxful of ribbons and honors for my paintings and many scrapbooks. I was the first woman exhibitor in the First National Indian Art Exhibition at the famed Philbrook Art Center, Tulsa, and won a purchase award. My paintings are in several national Indian museums in America and abroad. Most of the paintings in this book are in the collection of the Thomas Gilcrease Institute of American History and Art, Tulsa, Oklahoma.

One of my musical works, *Princess Ho-chee-nee's Song Album*, was released in 1971.

My life has been full of activities—always learning. My motto is, "Add something new to my 'brain-file' every day." This to me is as important as eating.

At the University of Tulsa, Professor Alexandra Hogue, the famous "sand-dune" painter, set my feet on a straight path with my Indian painting. Carlos Mérida, of the University of Mexico, pushed me along. Both said, "Do your own work. Follow no one." This I have done.

Six years of my life are in this book. All has been given to the Cherokee Foundation, Bartlesville, Oklahoma, with the hope that it will build a beautiful Indian Chapel in the Cherokee complex at Tahlequah, the first capital of the Cherokee Nation in Indian Territory.

We remember the brave thousands of vanquished Indians, robbed of all they possessed, driven like cattle in the dead of winter, some of the men in chains, children, women, all in a horrible struggle for survival with broken hearts for their lost homes and families, trying to reach Indian Territory, where they had been promised a haven of peace. More than a third were left to die beside the trail. All these we will remember in this memorial chapel.

We wish it could blot from the pages of American history this indelible stain of man's inhumanity to man.

JIMALEE BURTON
(Ho-chee-nee)

Sarasota, Florida
August 15, 1973

Acknowledgments

For assistance in preparation and publication of this book, I wish to extend acknowledgments and many thanks to:

William W. Keeler, Principal Chief, Cherokee Nation; Dr. Frederic J. Dockstader, Heye Foundation; Congressman James A. Haley and Mrs. Haley; William Jackson and the Selby Foundation; Mrs. Lois-Lee Parker; Dr. Emily Meadows; Mr. and Mrs. Elsworth Abbott; Mrs. Adam Stever; Mrs. Marion Godown; Miss Sally Lucke, Coordinator of Allied Arts, Sarasota County Schools, Sarasota County, Florida; and Mrs. Eudtia Teenor, Gilcrease Foundation.

The illustrations on the following pages are reproduced through the courtesy of the Thomas Gilcrease Institute of American History and Art, Tulsa, Oklahoma: pages 7, 10, 11, 29, 69, 77, 81, 84, 88, 89, 93, 104, 105, 109, 113, 128, 129, 132, 144, 148, 153, 156, and 160. The illustrations on the following pages are in the author's possession: pages 54, 72, 85, 97, 116, 117, and 121.

Contents

Color Illustrations

Indian Heritage, Indian Pride

The Ancestors

The Indians thought that the white men who came to their shores were gods descending from the sky or returning from the east. An ancient belief among the Indians was of a superior man with fair hair and white skin who had once lived among them and had taught them many things. They had been deeply grieved when he left, but he had promised to return.

When Columbus appeared, dressed in elaborate costume, with feather plumes waving from his hat, gold braid glittering in the sun, and a retinue of followers, the Indians were duly impressed. They were properly humble; they gave them food and their most precious gifts, with complete adoration as befitting a god. Thus they placed themselves at the mercy of these invaders, whose ambition was to take back to Spain the wealth that they were seeking and to win glory and honor as discoverers of a new world.

After his fortunate meeting with the Indians and his royal reception by them, Columbus wrote, "They know no religion, they are very intelligent, they love their neighbors as themselves and their speech is the sweetest and gentlest in the world." Everyone knows the stories of how the whites were fed and cared for when they first landed in the Americas. Yet, when the white men returned to Europe, they took with them as many natives as they could capture to sell as slaves, along with the finest treasures of the people. Many of the Indians died. They did not make willing slaves.

Not long after Columbus' voyages, other expeditions arrived from Europe. The men who remained to settle the New World stole Indian girls and women, trading them among themselves, treating them as necessities, not equals. Yet the Europeans had come face to face with a culture of great antiquity, with customs and principles in many ways superior to those that had evolved in Europe.

The Indians were not unlearned savages but a people whose foundation was as old as time. They were schooled in the laws of nature and had a profound religious belief in the creator of it all. The lust for gold, wracking disease, and the concept of land as individual property entered America with the white man.

Little did the colonists realize that they had encountered a people whose ancestors had built great civilizations, with knowledge of architecture, astronomy, and horticulture that has withstood the test of ages and mystified archaeologists, scientists, and thinkers down through time.

In my extensive travel and study in the Western Hemisphere, I visited the ancient masterpieces of a vanished people. I stood atop a high pyramid in Central America and gazed out over a vast area of crumbling walls and buildings decorated with fantastic carvings in the most intricate of patterns. I wondered, "Why was this civilization destroyed?" No answer came. I felt the tide of time wash over me.

Looking around, I saw the remains of a vast water system, paved streets, sculptures of dragons, serpents, birds, fish—all creatures of nature, as well as strange symbols like writing whose meanings have challenged the greatest scholars of modern times. From the clothing on the sculptured figures I judged their attire to have been as elaborate as the highly wrought architecture and carvings of the ancient buildings.

I looked again, trying to put my thoughts back in time, to visualize what a spectacle of grandeur this place must once have been. Some of the smaller foundations could have been great schools of learning, accounting houses, and courts of law. The government of these people

had to be a complex, well-organized system run by highly educated leaders to sustain their great achievements.

How long have the ancestors of the American Indian inhabited this hemisphere? No one knows. At Elk City, Oklahoma, an arrowhead was found imbedded in the bone of a prehistoric animal of an estimated age of 32,000 years. We can imagine that there were many changes in the earth's surface in those thousands of years. There may have been violent upheavals of nature, deadly changes in climate, or droughts that swept the builders of these ancient civilizations to their doom, leaving only remnants of survivors here and there to struggle back and re-establish themselves.

Such mysteries are not confined to the Americas. On the island of Oahu in Hawaii I saw, when the tide was low, tremendous walls of great stone that the tides of centuries have washed. I asked the native fishermen, "Who built those stone walls and why?" They answered, "The Gods," or, "The Little People." On Molokai are strange remnants of strong buildings reminding one of the Inca ruins I saw in the Andes Mountains in Peru. In my studies in Peru, Guatemala, Mexico, and Hawaii and on the Northwest Coast of North America, I found the same mysterious connecting links, suggesting that there was intercourse among the continents of the world in ancient times.

In my adopted state, Florida, archaeological discoveries are constantly being made. John Fales, who has an extensive collection of hieroglyphs, showed me a hieroglyphic plate he had unearthed in one of his Florida diggings. It was strikingly similar to symbols I had seen in Hawaii.

Ever since the white men first made contact with the Indians, historians, archaeologists, and scientists have been analyzing and writing about the origins of the Indians. Mormons in Utah told me that I was descended from the "Lost Tribes of Israel." Others claim Egyptian, African, and Oriental origins. Still others say that the Indians came to

Prayer

Great Spirit, whose tipi is the sky,
Whose hunting ground is the earth,
Mighty and fearful are you called.
Ruler over storm, over man, bird, and beast,
Over earthway, over skyway.
Find us this day our meat and corn
That we may be strong and brave.
Put aside from us our wicked ways,
As we put aside bad works of him who wrongs us.
Let us not be led onto troubled roads,
But keep us from all evil.
For yours is all that is—
The earth, the sky, streams and hills,
The stars, the moon, the sun—
All that lives and breathes.
Thou wonderful, shining,
Mighty, mighty Spirit.

The Contented Chieftain

the Americas from Asia on a land bridge across the Bering Strait. The last theory has the widest acceptance among scholars. Some of these analyses are well supported, tracing the Indian migration through the different ages. But to me it is all very simple—the Indians are a distinct people. They do not need "foreign" ancestors.

When we look at mountain and canyon strata, we can see tortured layer upon layer of rock. We know that this old world has been shaken up—probably many times. There could have been few survivors. I believe this happened in America. All people have traditional legends of a great flood. We can still see its effects. I have picked up seashells on mountaintops in several regions of Mexico and the West.

From a shale pit in Oklahoma my husband, Dan, took tons of shells, put them through a rock crusher, and used them in building a concrete roadbed for a highway from Collinsville to Claremore, Oklahoma. We found fossils in this shale, proving that parts of Oklahoma at one time were an ocean bed.

Adding all these things together, one can find it easy to believe that the natives the white explorers found in America were making a comeback. Tenaciously they had clung to their ancient customs and beliefs, to their respect for and worship of their creator. They represented the omnipotence of the Great Spirit with the sun symbol—the giver of life (the sun has been so worshiped at one time by every people of the world). The Indian will tell you that his ceremonies came from the Great Spirit, the one divine ruler whose spirit is in everything created by Him (page 7).

All Indian tribes have distinctive religious beliefs, handed down in meaningful rites from their ancestors. All these rituals were performed to assure spiritual renewal, health, peace, and prosperity. How could white men understand a people whose rituals, refined over centuries, seemed so different from their own? The invaders, in their ignorance, judged the Indians to be "uneducated savages." Since until recent years the white man has been the "historian," this image of the Indian has been perpetuated among the American people. In many eyes the Indian is viewed at worst as a heathen and at best as a mystery.

Nor did the Indians understand white men or their lack of respect for life. To them the white man is not satisfied with this beautiful, bountiful world. He wants to remake it to suit himself, and yet he does not know what he wants. That attitude has been reinforced by government policies which have had the effect of destroying both the white and the red man's opportunity to learn the best from each race, as one people advancing in all knowledge in harmony. The Indian—even he whose blood is mixed with that of whites—is proud to be an Indian and to claim it before the world. And, of course, many enlightened white people accept it as a compliment if one says, "You look like an Indian." They may then tell you of ancestors who had Indian blood.

There is no way to estimate the numbers of Indians living in the Americas when the white men arrived. Ethnologists have estimated the population at about one million in North America, three to four million in Mexico and Central America, and perhaps as many in South America. Whatever their numbers, they proved no match for the predatory colonizers from the east. After constant persecution, dispersal, and displacement, their power to defend their land was broken, and the tribes were destroyed, decimated, or assimilated and, in what is now the continental United States, imprisoned on reservations in the West. Ashes were raked over their council fires.

Yet the surviving Indians retained their pride. That is one of the wonders of the world. Through more than 450 years of pressure employed in every way that could be devised, the government has tried to make them over. It has placed Indian children in boarding schools and kept them for as long as eight years of white men's education and culture. In such schools they are seldom taught about their ancestors and the contributions made by them to the Western world. Yet in such a climate their determination is often astonishing. I have seen many an Indian girl, returning from school, get off the train dressed in her con-

The Prisoner and *The Judge*

The ancient Aztec Indians were a superior people who created a remarkable culture in the Valley of Mexico. Then, laid waste by Spanish conquerors, their civilization was virtually destroyed.

Very little of Aztec culture remains to us today. But we know that they were remarkable artisans and architects. The grace and beauty of their archi-

tecture have never been surpassed. What remains is being carefully excavated by archaeologists.

In a few protected places are remnants of murals decorating broken and cracked walls, but still retaining some of their brilliant colors. My visit to the ruins inspired these two paintings, done in the style of the ancient Aztecs.

The symbols on the wall before the judge represent his words as he offers a choice of punishments to the prisoner.

ventional school clothes, happily greet her blanketed Indian parents, take a blanket, and put it around her, in that proudly symbolic fashion reassuming her Indian ways.

Yet after Indians spend a few years in white schools, the shock of adjusting to the old life may be enormous. They are misfits. Their families have no money; their people do not understand them. Their fortitude to meet life on Indian terms has been weakened. The ambition of many of them is to help their people—but how? With no direction, their culture and religious beliefs undermined, they are easy prey for the white man's ills—sad the ending of years away from home.

Yet, with the persecution and the subjugation by the whites, the Indians have managed to retain much of their heritage. They are mystics by nature: among the Zuñis a "poor man" is one who has no spiritual knowledge; a "wealthy man" is one versed in the "spiritual wonders of his ancestors." One who speaks with sympathy and understanding of the Indians' past, their perception of nature and life, is called romantic and unrealistic. Yet theirs was not a superficial concept of values. Ultimately the things that had meaning for them were spiritual, not material, proceeding in religious simplicity profound in import, they spoke from the heart:

The ones who hold high places,
Once more assuming human form,
Sat down quietly at the Sacred Place,
Spreading out their mist blanket,
They sent forth their life-giving road,
Carrying their waters,
Carrying their seeds,
They made the roads go forth.

When I was a student of Indian art and history in Mexico, a professor of archaeology at the University of Mexico and I made many explorations of the ruins of San Juan Teotihuacán, the great Pyramids of the

Sun and the Moon. There we were in another world (see pages 10 and 11).

It was said the buildings were originally covered with colored tile inscribed with hieroglyphs. Glistening in the Mexican sun, it must have been a beautiful sight to the people going about their daily work up and down the wide avenues of the ancient city. One feels a baffling, bewildering mystery among these magnificent ruins; one's imagination can run riot.

On one visit I saw some women with several children digging in an excavation pit. I hurried over to see what they had uncovered, and a little pile of artifacts caught my eye. Looking closer, I saw fascinating small heads and busts of people—all kinds of people. Some were made of fired clay, and some seemed to have been carved from stone. Never had we seen anything like them. On this spot could have stood the studio of an ancient artist. Strange their headdresses, strange their clothes, but very familiar their faces. Here were features we might see every day, in any city—Arab, Chinese, Mongolian, Jew, black—one could not mistake them; they were clearly indicated. They were portraits in sculptured clay and stone, made by professional artists, buried in antiquity. I bought a dozen or so but did not realize the importance of my find at the time.

Later I spent three months at Ajijic, a small Indian village on Lake Chapala, near Guadalajara. There I studied Spanish with Dolores, an Aztec-Spanish beauty about eighteen years old. I became fascinated by the romantic, tragic stories Dolores told of the ancient customs of her people and her family (her father had been the head of a private college and had been murdered during a revolution). I learned that her stories had formed the base for two books by American writers.

Dolores said that many small heads similar to those I had bought at Teotihuacán had been found in Lake Chapala, hidden there along with treasures of gold, jewels, and priceless artifacts. Evidently they had been placed there during some great invasion. Some of the families of Ajijic and other villages around the lake had found the treasures, which had made them wealthy.

Legend says that the region around Lake Chapala was the seat of a great civilization that was destroyed by earthquake and flood. Many stories are told of how the people prayed that the water would disappear and made sacrifices to the God of Waters. Babies were placed on a well-like altar, while the people begged for their lives as the little ones cried in terror and were finally covered by the rising tide. It is also said many small carved heads were cast into the waters with the prayers.

The natives of Lake Chapala were probably destroyed, but others of their people have survived many catastrophes—imposed by nature and by man—down through eons of time.

The Indian and the American Government

The Bureau of Indian Affairs is a most efficient octopus, reaching into the lives and homes of most American Indians. Some important officials of the BIA still mistakenly believe that they, as representatives of a superior race and protectors of an inferior race, have broad powers which need no explanation. Their authoritative orders are law. These officials are still feared by their employees and by the Indians under their jurisdiction. They do not believe in Indian self-government, for such is a threat to their power and authority.

Few in government want to listen to the Indian. Long ago he learned that his voice is seldom heard. The attitude taken toward him by his "protectors" is degrading and bewildering. He gets what the BIA wants him to have.

This experience with the government, which also fosters suspicion among the tribes, and even among his own people, through favoritism and bribery as a means of buying good will, has all but destroyed his faith in humanity. He suspects that he can trust no one.

The BIA still operates on the theory that the Indians are unable to govern their own affairs either as individuals or as groups. The bureau clings to the conviction that it must direct and control, that it alone knows what is best for the Indians, until such time as they reach a "higher plane," when control will be handed over to them.

This vision of directing the Indian toward a goal of self-government is so inspiring—and so profitable—to the thousands of bureau employees that they will not willingly give it up. Many really are not interested in the welfare of the Indians. Without the Indians what would happen to the bureau?

In the United States, "the land of the free," the Indian is not free. Our heritage is freedom, but we are not free. We are told that we are unable to run our own affairs because we do not have the necessary education. Whose fault is that? Schools specifically designed for the education of Indian children have been among our chief desires. Some of the Indian-oriented schools are merely token showcases, organized to lull Indians into believing that they are getting an education.

One school on the Zuñi Reservation had the same teacher for almost twenty years. When a friend of mine, with another teacher, took charge of it, she said: "The children had never been taught English. They were allowed to do just what they pleased, 'playing at school.' " They learned more in the first semester she was there than earlier students had learned in all the twenty previous years. She told how eager the children were to learn.

The Indian is still chained hand and foot, waiting for the fulfillment of promises often made but never kept. This overwhelming tide of "civilization" has practically passed the Indian by, while the government welcomes strangers from all over the world. Scores of immigrants are taken in, sent to school, taught English, given jobs. Churches graciously take whole families under their wing, give them homes, help them achieve security and prosperity. We see across the land prosperous settlements of the foreign-born, still practicing their own native customs and faiths. They are respected and welcomed into American society. A man of foreign birth said to me: "Why worry about the Indians? They have got it good. The government takes care of them, gives them a place to live, schools, hospitals and money. Why don't they forget they are Indians and be like other people?" Such ignorance would be amusing if it were not so deplorably sad, so typical of the white man's view.

In America the distorted image of the Indian as barbarian and savage by greedy white settlers and politicians has been perpetuated down through the years, not because the Indian was in fact inferior physically, mentally, or morally but because he was an Indian with the distinct characteristics of his race and because the Indian owned this fabulous country, whose riches were sought from the time of its discovery by whites. Is it not time to stop imposing the false stereotype and offer whites an accurate picture of Indian culture and history?

Take any race of people in the world, isolate them for generations on poor land, allow them firewater to dull their senses and stifle their ambition, deny them any opportunity for advancement, let them survive or perish with less than subsistence resources, and what would be the outcome? I maintain that the Indian has proved he is a man of character and of "long thoughts" to survive such treatment.

The Bureau of Indian Affairs, under the supervision of the Department of the Interior since 1849, was organized to control or eliminate the Indians. It did just that. In the bloody, gloomy days of Indian-white confrontation, white sentiment was overwhelmingly against the Indian. The only solution was to let bullets do the work, cover up the bloody deeds, and say no more. God and humanity were forgotten.

Something had to be done to get the Indians out of the settlers' way, eliminating them by every means, moving them from place to place, farther and farther west as the invaders advanced. The Indians at last were completely frustrated, their people starving and suffering untold hardships. Everything they had was gone. Whole tribes died from white men's bullets and contagious diseases. At last they were forced onto reservations. Then smart politicians in the government and the bureau began to realize what a plum they had in the Indians. They decided to make them wards of the bureau. In that way they could keep the land and the Indians in their power. Many Indian tribes actually paid for their land (which was already theirs), hoping for a place of safety. Yet the bureau has maintained supervision, even to this day. This bureau has grown over the years until now it is a giant of power, among the richest in Washington, D.C. It is a national disgrace in this "land of the free."

It is said that no land treaty between the American government and the Indians has been honored. Occasionally one reads of an Indian tribe winning a court suit against the United States government for land taken. Though the settlement may run to thousands of dollars, little money is left for the Indians after the government charges off its services to them and the lawyers are paid.

The reservations are usually land that Uncle Sam does not want. Much of it will not support a horse or a cow. If there happens to be a fertile spot, eventually a farmer or a cattleman will take it over on a rental agreement with the bureau. The Indian seldom gets the proceeds. He lives on the side of a hill and watches. Sad his eyes, hungry his belly.

The great western artist Charles M. Russell lived with the Indians for years as an Indian. He wrote: "This is a land of thirst, it belongs to the "Injuns," nobody is going to take it from him for a while, Uncle Sam is mighty good that way—anything he can't use he lets the Injuns keep."

Besides the millions of dollars appropriated by the government for bureau use, the bureau exercises control over practically all funds belonging to the tribes, except perhaps money earned by their own efforts. If they invest those earnings in a house on the reservation, that, too, in some cases, comes under bureau control.

Every year the bureau collects a tremendous amount of income from mineral, forest, and water rights and even income from Indian property. The bureau has the right to review or approve most actions of tribal governing bodies in regard to management of assets belonging to the tribe. This amounts to billions of dollars, which goes to the BIA to support the Indian Affairs program, especially to support its many thousands of employees and equipment. Soon there may be more employees than Indians. Once while attending a "Western Day Celebration" parade in Fairbanks, Alaska, I saw two white tourists. They, supposing I was a native, began talking with me, telling me about the fun they were having on this vacation, while making a survey of the health of the Indians and Eskimos of Alaska for the BIA. When I said, "I am from Oklahoma, and a member of the National Congress of American Indians," they drifted away. It would be interesting to know how many fine vacations are enjoyed each year by BIA employees, on Indian money.

The lack of cooperation of the bureau with the Indian on any project leaves him hopeless and at the mercy of the agents who tell him what to do. I have seen Indians rich in oil lands declared incompetent. They had only what the bureau allowed them.

I recall my interest in a little Navajo mission. The Indians wanted to construct a small building to house a chapel and three hospital beds for patients. The Indians said that they would build it of native stone and do all the work if the bureau would furnish material for windows, doors, roof, and interior. They would install everything themselves. The bureau decided that a Quonset hut without interior finish would do. That is what the Indians got—in cold, snowy country—for hospital beds. The missionary (an Indian) wrote to me: "For their Christmas dinner the people of the mission had baked beans, apples, nuts, canned peaches, and cake made with raisins. They had no meat. But they were thankful for what they had. Some had walked for miles in the snow with their feet wrapped in rags to get here."

Down through the years the BIA has kept the Indian in ignorance, despair, and a state of fear. I remember in years past that if a tribe's actions did not please the BIA payment of their small allotment would be withheld—payment for land taken by treaty. In some cases the agent kept the money for his own use; the Indian starved. Yet just suppose what would happen today if the Social Security Administration told the millions of whites on their rolls, "If you don't do as we say, we will withhold your social security payments," as though they had no right to their own money.

In the early days in Oklahoma many Indians had nothing to live on but a small government allotment, as little as ten or fifteen dollars quarterly. Everything they had had was gone. They were not trained to work for money; all they knew was trade and hunt, and after the settlers came, hunting was not good, and there was nothing to trade.

Despite the appropriations made by the government for the BIA program for the Indians and the revenue from the reservations, Indian properties, and mineral rights, I doubt that more than 10 per cent is ever returned to the reservations.

There are Indian employees in the BIA, but their voices are weak. Though they may not agree with BIA policy, to keep their positions, they say little.

To dominate a race of people, do not educate them; educated people ask questions. Make them believe that everything you do is for their good. Encourage them to live the Indian life and work at their crafts. Indian crafts are being promoted by the bureau today. In fact, the BIA took over an academic Indian school in Santa Fe, New Mexico, and turned it into a school of art because they found Indian art valuable and therefore much more important than the education of children. I wonder how anyone can make a living beading a pair of moccasins, weaving a rug, or painting a picture at the price a tourist will pay an Indian. The Indians want the good things in life, just as their white brothers do. They do not want to sit in a shack lighted by oil lamps and carry their water for miles, while they watch the white man drive by on the fine roads built with Indian money.

A couple of tourists, talking about a recent trip through a western Indian reservation, spoke of buying an unusual Navajo rug. They were delighted that it cost so little but shocked when they learned that the weavers lived in the brush arbor and shack where they were working. It was their home—all they had. The tourists asked: "How do they live in such a place? It was most picturesque, with the bright rugs about and the women in their colorful Navajo dress. But to live there! It was awful! We could hardly believe it. One woman was in the yard, dying yarn, cooking it in a big black iron pot. She said: 'We card, spin, and make our own yarn and then dye it like this.' Two young girls were winding bright-colored yarn. Later, when we asked a man if these weavers live there all the year, he said, 'Yes.' "

It takes much time and hard work to weave a rug, shearing the sheep for the wool, washing, carding, spinning the yarn, and then dying it. Some of the dyes are made in the old way, from herbs and roots. Afterward come the long hours of weaving the ancient patterns into something lasting and beautiful. Then the tourists arrive to haggle and bargain for a lower price. It is no wonder that some of these reservation Indians have the lowest incomes of any people in the United States —as low as three hundred dollars a year. Indians cannot achieve even a modest standard of living, much less the beautiful things of life (and they love beautiful things too, as shown by their art and clothing) with crafts alone.

Even genuine Indian arts are endangered. The modern age is fast sweeping away the very qualities that have made Indian art unique. Today art students are encouraged to prostitute the traditional symbols, which expressed deep religious feeling and served as an outlet for their love of beauty and natural concepts of color harmony, reflecting the sky and the earth and all it contains. This distinct art may well soon be lost, its character "modernized" and swallowed up in a sort of "homogenizing" tide that destroys its uniqueness. One is fortunate who has an opportunity to acquire a concept of the true art, fast disappearing with the drive toward assimilation.

The invasion of Indian lands has been unremitting. It still goes on today—carried on by government developers and politicians out to fleece the Indian of the last place he has. They have a clever idea: "Make the Indian think he is in big business." But they do not fool the Indians.

It sounds fine to tourists: "Go fishing with the Apaches." They load up the children, their cans of beer, and visit the reservation. Then away they go, leaving their blight wherever they have been.

Engineers with their tripods and bulldozers are swarming all over the reservations. The valleys where the Indians' cattle grazed, where his little home was sheltered by the mountains—all gone, the crystal-clear waters of the meandering streams he loved now impounded by great dams of earth and cement. When the Indian objects, he is told: "This is progress. You will get a fine job and make plenty of money." The Indian does not want this. He has begged and prayed for industry and businesses on the reservation, but industry and businesses he can own and operate himself. It seems to him that anything the Indians start on their own is discouraged.

White workmen take the "fine jobs." The Indians dig the ditches. They man some of the concessions and boat docks, act as guides, and maybe dress in a warbonnet to pose for photographs. But the Indians do not own the concessions—the BIA agents collect the rent. Everybody benefits from the Indians' money and their land but the Indians. They dig the ditches.

Smart politicians encourage the selection of young men with a drop or so of Indian blood for training, to inveigle the protesting Indians into following the line, like the bell goat in a herd of sheep. The Indians cannot win.

Public schools are being built for white children on the reservations. The Indians can attend these schools, but they want their own, fearing that they will forget their traditions, their language, everything that has given them fortitude down through the years. The Great Spirit watches; he must weep with the Indians.

Such tactics are not confined to the reservations in the West. The Menominee Indians in Wisconsin managed to build their own sawmill to harvest the timber on their reservation. They had a going business. The BIA did not approve and in 1961 pushed through Congress a termination bill. The reservation, sawmill, everything was turned over to a white corporation. The Indian stock of 48,000 shares was placed in trust. The trust company has the right to vote this minority stock. A large new development company was organized. Immediately it began selling the land.

Such tactics left the Menominees helpless and jobless. It is a sad sight to see the way some of them live: in shacks made of scrap and junk, in old cars. The years of "development" have about finished the Indians.

Politicians and promoters, with their godless technology and diabolic machines, tear away at the earth in a mad rush to change it. "You can't stop progress!" they cry.

The reservations are steadily being invaded, eroded.

How long, how long can this last?

God's drum is booming!

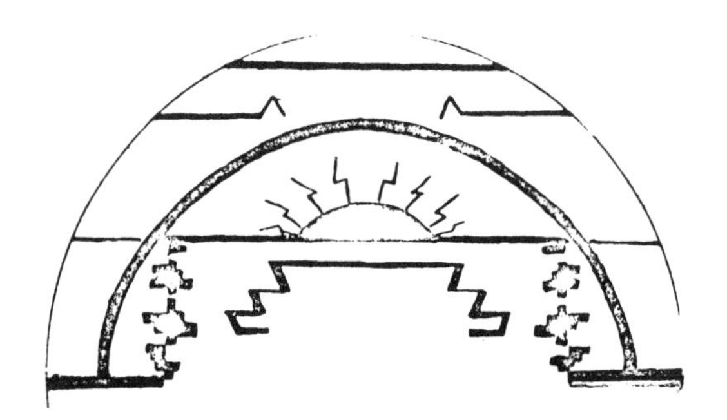

The Old Ones Weep

A crimson-glowing sky, behind darkening clouds of night that glide across the heavens in a silent symphony of glory. The sun is gone. Mystic forms take shape, drawn by the sure hand of the Master Designer on his endless sky canvas.

We thrill to the spirit presence, remembering . . . this is where the First Americans found many of their sacred symbols for their art. Here they found inspiration for their soul-cleansing ceremonies, rituals to bring them closer to the one Great Spirit of all harmony.

"The white man thinks with his head—the Indian thinks with his heart." This difference is expressed by the Indian in song and in daily ritual from birth to death. In the spring the Indian sings, "Walk carefully; Mother Earth is pregnant."

The young Indian thrust into white society is confused by the lack of respect for divine values. His way of life is completely turned around. Everywhere he sees heartless destruction and is told that it is progress. He sees his beloved Mother Earth fighting a losing battle to heal the gaping wounds inflicted by whining bulldozer and piercing drill.

The Indian heart pounds in agony. Nature's children, his little brothers, are dying, gasping for breath. Must he say, "Good-by forever," to the clear bubbling spring, the great trees that have lived with the ages, the coyote's night song, the echo from the mountain across a peaceful, sweet-smelling, dew-drenched valley, under a starlit night? The Indian cries with them.

The Indian does not like what he sees—people huddled in cities, isolated from life's sustaining elements, hating each other, systematically fed and housed, afraid to be alone, pacified and directed by the incessant TV and anesthetized by the news, their brain waves clogged with trash, while concentrated sound waves bombard their bodies. The children grow tall but weak, members of a faceless society, trying vainly to find an answer for itself.

The urban Indian is caught up in a dizzy whirl of speed, greed, drugs, sex. Confused, he yearns to sit under a tree and think. No one understands him. "Be like us!" the whites cry. At length, with his values all but destroyed, sadly he returns to his people. They love him, but they do not understand. He has lost his sacred identity with the place the Great Spirit has allotted to him.

Indian hearts and eyes are sad. Where can he hide? We read, "Indian Youth Commits Suicide."

The old ones weep.

The Medicine Man

A medicine man was consecrated to his calling from birth. He was a person set apart. He learned to sense the place where thoughts come from, to listen to the voice of nature in the blue flatness of the sky and in the roar of thunder, to lose himself in silence and hear the Great Spirit in his heart and the gentle whisper of the wind. He heard the sounds of nature with each changing season—the exploding of reborn spring, the tingling heat of summer sun, the dropping of autumn leaves blanketing the earth to keep it warm in winter. The wisdom of a true medicine man was profound.

I remember the daughter of a prominent Indian family who was sent to a finishing school in the East. While she was there, she had a nervous breakdown. Her parents, accepting white man's ways, put her under the care of the best doctors. Their verdict: They could do nothing for her. The parents then decided to follow the Indian way. Off she went to the reservation, where she was left with a famous old medicine man. With the aid of his gentle philosophy and medicinal herbs before long the girl was completely well and happy, returning home cured. She had learned how to meet life the Indian way.

Many years ago a decorator was doing some work in my home. In the middle of the job he announced that he could not return for several days. His wife was scheduled for a serious operation—removal of a cancerous breast.

The Four Aspects of Life

When treating a patient, the Indian medicine man found power in the secret place of meditation. With patience and understanding he analyzed and prescribed, to bring each aspect of life to perfect harmony of being—to feel the place where happiness is, to find full strength and perfect rhythm. Often he performed miraculous cures.

The painting shows (beginning in the lower left corner):

A child is born.
He walks life's road,
From childhood to youth,
From youth to manhood,
From manhood to old age.
Each tangent a road turn.
The last road finished,
Again he joins Earth Mother.
His spirit flies beyond the sky
To the place of long abiding
With the Great Spirit of all.

HO-CHEE-NEE
JIMALEE BURTON

A few days later he returned to work, looking carefree and happy.

"How is your wife?" I asked.

"She is just fine!"

"So the operation went all right?"

"I'll say it did! She didn't have it. Our neighbors persuaded me to take my wife to Salina, Oklahoma, to an Indian medicine man. The doctor was furious, but we canceled the operation.

"We saw lots of people there and heard amazing things, while waiting for the medicine man. One woman said, 'See that man standing there? He's my husband. We brought him here in a wheelchair. He had not walked in eleven years. I told this medicine man that if he would make my husband walk I'd give him a thousand dollars. Look at him walking now! He feels fine. We are so happy!' "

I said to the decorator, "What did he do for your wife?"

"He stirred up some dark-looking salve, put it on and covered it with a pad. 'This will be very painful,' he said, 'but under no circumstances remove it.' When we returned for our appointment, the medicine man removed the pack. The growth lifted out."

The last time I heard from the patient she was well.

The medical profession and ignorant people ridicule the medicine man. But we know what we know. Natural penicillin and many other so-called great scientific discoveries were used by our Indian ancestors thousands of years before the white man reached America. Being students of nature, they sought and found cures in her boundless riches, guided by the power of the Great Spirit. With their sense of consecration they made many cures, solved many mysteries. The medicine man of today retains this attitude of consecration. But he does not speak of his cures or tell his secrets, lest they lose their power (see page 29).

Ironically, no Indian medicine man is allowed to practice medicine, even though he may have studied—earned a degree in medicine in a white man's university, as had the one at Salina. He was barred from practicing, despite the pleadings of the people he had cured.

The Indian Hunter
Addresses a Deer He Has Slain

I am sorry to kill thee, little brother;
But I had need of thy meat:
My children were crying for food.
Forgive me, little brother.
I will do honor to thy courage,
Strength, and beauty—see.
I will hang thy horns on this tree;
Each time I pass I will remember,
And do honor to thy spirit.
I am sorry I had to kill thee;
Forgive me, little brother.
See, I smoke to thy memory,
I burn tobacco.

*Earth**

I am Earth.
A divine testament.
I am the mother of all man.
For me the stars shine.
The sun stokes my heart flame,
The wind, my life breathing.
Behold the blue sky tabernacle;
My sacred kiva.
O man, walk carefully.
I am your mother.

* Originally published in *Defenders of Wildlife News* (Washington, D.C., 1971).

A Race with a River

Mary and Jim Chitwood—my mother and father—loved to tell about Indian Territory days. Those stories were so real and exciting to me that even today when I think of them I feel as though I had been there and lived them too. I have a right to feel that way; I grew up in western Oklahoma, where the events took place.

My father's trading post was a meeting place for all kinds of people, from the best to the worst. Most of them were newcomers to Indian country. Of course, Father had Indian customers too, who, like mother, were there when the white men came. My father was part-Irish. I am sure his ancestors kissed the blarney stone; when he talked, everybody listened.

You may have heard the trite saying, "An Indian never forgets." That was my mother. When Oklahoma began to race along the road to progress and one of my parents' enterprising acquaintances became successful in the government, Father would laugh when Mother would whisper, "That old horse thief." She really knew who was who in western Oklahoma—she never forgot.

My husband, Dan, often said, "Never go to your mother's house without your notebook. She is a fountain of information." I was careless about taking his advice but I remember the stories my parents told.

Once when Jim and Mary had been married only a short time, they went on a trip that took them across the treacherous Canadian River, south of El Reno. It was an outlaw river. Its sandy bed was a half mile or so wide, with only a narrow channel running through it during the dry season. The channel changed its course every spring when the waters rose. That was when people feared the river. Down thundered the water, threatening everyone who dared live in the valley. The Indians did not trust the river. When the ranchers came to the Canadian River country in the spring, they worried about their cattle. Some said, "The water rises right up out of the sand." One day the riverbed would be dry, the next a raging sea.

High water was not the only danger the Canadian River held. Here and there were quicksand beds, threatening a terrible death for an unsuspecting person or animal that stopped to take a drink of water.

Now Jim and Mary were returning home from their trip and recrossing the river. Jim loved fine horses and was proud of his horse and buggy—his "rig," he called it. Mary called it "my chariot."

They were taking it easy. The sand was dry and hard. It was spring, the early-blooming time of the year. The cottonwood trees were shaking their puffs of cotton on the air; the willows were coming out in golden-tinted green. Mother Earth was stirring and urging on the awakening new life bursting within her. From their hideaways animals and birds were peeping curiously as the buggy passed. Not many people came this way in the early days.

Mary had been telling Jim about her childhood experiences—going with her brothers for dry wood, which they had to have to start their fires. Now she was singing to Jim out of joy in the beautiful spring day.

They had just begun crossing the river when they saw an Indian riding along in a great hurry. He stopped and said. "Children, go home quick. River is coming. I go tell people."

Quickly they started across the riverbed, their hearts beating fast with the speeding horses. It was a wild ride, but they made it across the channel. Looking up the river, they could see the flood of water tumbling over the sand, pushing everything before it. It was an awesome sight. Had they been caught on the other side of the river, there would have been no crossing for many days, and they without shelter or food.

But why think of such things? It was a beautiful day. Mary began singing again, as they continued across the riverbed.

Then suddenly they heard an ominous roar. What is that? They looked up. There was not a cloud in the sky. But a sense of great danger gripped them. Looking up the river, they saw to their horror a great wall of water! The horses, Dick and Pat, saw it, too, and with Jim's excited cluck and command and the snap of the lines they knew what they had to do. Forward they leaped, pulling the buggy, racing across the sand. Jim knew that if they were caught in the middle of that seething caldron, they could die buried in the dreaded quicksand and never be found. Mary held on tight, outwardly calm, but her heart pounding.

Jim yelled, "Mary, pray!"

Closer came the mad river, crushing, foaming, sweeping all before it. They could hear the crack and crash of trees and bushes as they folded into broken, twisted masses, tossed like straws into the sand, hitting it with such force that it swirled up to meet the oncoming sea. Mary was praying. She knew that only God and their two fine horses could save them. On they flew, Jim urging the panting horses, "On! On!" Closer, closer came the river. Now it was lapping at the wheels. Faithful Dick and Pat were straining every muscle. Everything depended on them, and they knew it. Now the water was reaching the bed of the buggy. Mary asked God to help Dick and Pat. She asked God to hold back the fearsome wall of water. She recalled how God had saved the children of Israel when Moses was leading them out of Egypt—how the Red Sea parted and let them walk to safety. Mary believed.

Jim was talking to the horses to keep them from panic. Then, glory be, they found a firm footing. Up the bank they went to dry ground. They had made it!

Dick and Pat came to a stop, snorting and blowing, shaking all over from their ordeal. Jim looked at Mary. She said, "Don't worry about me. I'm all right." Jim jumped out of the buggy and hurried to the heaving horses, patting them and talking to them to calm their fears. Mary sat for a bit, thanking God for their delivery, and then joined Jim to thank the horses for saving their lives. A true Indian never forgets to honor the animals, his little brothers, for their help and courage. They are part of the divine plan of Mother Earth, who sustains us all.

Days of Yesterday

Yesterday, stories of yesterday, I learned from my parents—the yesterday of the First American, the Indian, the cowboy, and the settlers. I saw them all at the trading post.

Pony-express riders, covered wagons, stagecoaches, great cattle drives—my father was there, exploring that exhilarating, exciting new country. Leaving his father's home in Tennessee as a lad of fifteen, riding his pony with a six-shooter at his side, over hundreds of miles of virgin country he made his way to Colonel Charles Goodnight's ranch in the Panhandle-Plains country of Texas. Later he went to Indian Territory and opened a trading post. It took him months to make it, but he made it—he was a young man who "went west." In his stories I lived those days too.

In the yesterdays of Oklahoma the trading post was the crossroads of the locality—Indians, white people, all kinds of people came to look or trade and passed on. It was a little cross section of a very big country, where anything could—and did—happen.

That is where we learned many things, when we didn't know we were learning. The store with people coming to trade—talking, visiting. The drummers won my friendship with small samples of their merchandise or a deposit in my money bank. A little ruby-red glass pitcher given to me is now a collector's item.

Our house was near the store. As soon as I was big enough to trot around, I tagged after Father and loved to be in the store. A pet coyote was our little dog. "God's dog," Father said. One time we really got into trouble. Coyote found the shelf of cotton batting. What a mess he made, making himself a cozy bed! Father was mad. Coyote was banned from the store.

It was the time of year when people began wearing long underwear and coats. A big old pot-bellied stove stood in the back of the store, and around it the men who weren't in a hurry would sit and "gas." A man got up, opened the door of the stove to spit out a chaw of tobacco. Out went his false teeth with the cud, right into the fire! All the men were hollering and laughing. I guess it was pretty funny to them, but I, being just a little girl, was sorry for the poor man. Now I think that it must have been pretty funny. That man was the joke around the store.

When I was big enough to sit a pony, father taught me to ride western style. All over the ranch the hunting hounds and I tagged him. By the time I was seven, I was a pretty good rider. What fun we had! I learned the way the squirrel barks and practiced bird calls. I learned the quail call and the turkey call, but I could not learn to use the turkey caller as well as Father did. Every time we were out we found something new to talk about. Do you know that the drumming of the woodpecker makes a perfect rhythm? He is "God's kettle drummer." The coyote really sings; he doesn't "howl" except for a special reason, such as sending a message to his brothers. The rattlesnake doesn't want to bite you. He is scared, just as you are of him.

A world of information was part of me before my school days. I was taught like an Indian, living close to the earth with wonderful, thinking, nature-loving parents. It all came naturally, with much joy of learning, when I didn't know I was learning.

We were hunting wild plums in the big pasture, Mother, my sister, Maudelia, and I, when we found a nest of baby birds right in the top of a low bush. Their little backs were red from the hot sun. Resourceful Mother soon fixed that with a nice little brush tipi she built over them. As we were leaving, the mother bird was already with them.

I learned about money from going to the bank with Father. How proud I was of my little bankbook and my deposits!

One day Father said, "Ho-chee-nee, you know where money is?"

"Yes, Papa."

"Now listen to me and don't forget. If you ever lose your money, don't tell anyone, but go to a bank. Tell them you want to see the president. Don't talk to a flunkie. Tell the president who you are, that you are my daughter. He will see that you get money." This good advice I have followed many times.

When I graduated to a gay little pony called Pompey, who wanted to play and would dance around, Mother would worry. "Jim, you will get that child killed."

Papa would call to me, "Chee-nee, use your quirt." I learned to be boss. Pompey loved me.

Before I had learned to plait my long hair, Father took me with him on a buying trip for the store, to Kansas City, Missouri. My hair was a problem until he turned me over to his barber. He fixed it just like Mother did. In those days the wholesale dealers gave presents to their customers. I came home with some pretty clothes, boots, leggings, a coat, and a beautiful bisque doll with natural hair that I could comb and eyes that went to sleep. I kept that doll always. It was the favorite of all my dolls.

If we are taught to observe and use our five senses, we will find distinct odors all about us. I think few people realize how important their "smellers" really are. Many people are surrounded with cigarette smoke and actually cannot smell. I remember one time I was close to a rattlesnake. I smelled him before I saw him, coiled and ready to strike. I had time to get away, just because I smelled him.

The store was a fascinating place. You could shut your eyes and know exactly where you were in the store just by the smell. From the pungent smell of the cured hides in their special house you passed the drums of coal oil in the shed, used for stoves, lamps, and many things;

through the grocery department, with its barrels of sauerkraut and pickles, the big round of cheese with the cleaver above it ready for cutting—everything had a decided smell. A fine lunch of crackers, cheese, a can of tomatoes, and maybe a can of peaches made a fine treat for many a hungry traveler or shopper. The Indian traders always made a picnic.

Then there was the coffee grinder, with the bags of good-smelling coffee. Some people bought the green coffee and roasted it themselves. All the children especially liked the candy case. It was fun to see how many real-looking things were made in candy—the little tin skillets with the natural-looking fried egg; the red, white, and blue American flags; horehound sticks, peppermint sticks, gummy gumdrops, natural-looking yellow corn that even fooled the chickens. Then the smell of gunpowder in the shells by the gun case; the smell of good leather in saddles, harness, boots, and shoes. Always something to think about.

In the front of the store were the dress goods and clothing. Different colors and materials have different odors. We always noticed that when the boxes of new goods were being unpacked. Father was a judge of quality and taught me to know material just by feeling and smelling.

We think of checked tablecloths as being old-fashioned. In those yesterdays the Indians bought yards of it, and unbleached sheeting too, to make summer shawls. The men wore them around their waists. They were very handy for carrying things and other purposes—they even made a good sunshade on a hot day.

I loved the days when the Indians came to the store to trade, when they received their allotments from the government. These were payments for ceded land, not gifts. It wasn't much, I remember. Parked behind the store were the covered wagons with tipi poles tied on the side. They always took their overnight homes with them if they had to travel far. All of them enjoyed this get-together day, for shopping and visiting. The men would be sitting around, in their blankets if the weather was cool, swapping stories, some on the long veranda in front of the store, their western hats pulled down over their eyes, the older ones with string-wrapped braids. You never heard loud, boisterous laughter among Indians. They had lots of fun but always behaved with poise and dignity when in public.

The full-blood Indians were hairless except for their heads. What few hairs they had on their faces they pulled. I thought nothing of it then, but I do remember now seeing them using their tweezers while sitting around. The prettiest hands I have ever seen have been those of the Indians. They are usually small and well formed, as are their feet, which they used to care for by oiling them.

Indian women and children too enjoyed these shopping get-togethers. If you have ever seen Indian babies, you know how cunning and bright they are. The young babies had long black hair; they looked like little dolls. (Mother had a little braid that she kept among her "keepsakes"; it was my first baby hair.)

Indian babies were carefully trained from the time they entered the new life. They were never allowed to cry. The mother would gently put her fingers on the baby's little windpipe, while softly singing or talking. She would press just enough to let him know he was not to cry. He soon learned. This was done for his protection; an outcry might betray his presence.

I remember a story told of a baby being found hidden under a basket after a massacre in which most of the Indians of a village were murdered. It had lain there under the basket with no outcry, even though it had a bullet hole through one arm, until it was discovered, hidden there by its protecting mother, who lost her life.

I have seen babies begging to be put in their carrying cradle. They loved to be in their own little cozy nest, an instinct natural to every living thing.

I was just a little girl, but in my memory remains a beautiful picture I think of as the "Covered Wagon Madonna." I have made several sketches, and one day it will materialize. I was visiting among the covered wagons parked back of the store, when a pretty Indian woman smiled at me. She was sitting on the front seat of a covered wagon. I climbed up on the spokes of the wheel, and there on her lap was a little baby laughing and cooing while its mother was giving it a bath. Beside her was a tin of water. The mother would take a mouthful of water, hold it a minute, then squirt it over the baby, and wipe it off. How that baby was enjoying its warm bath!

What a precious gift is memory—a built-in storehouse to open at will. On life's screen we see the building blocks of all the things that have touched us to enrich our perception and evaluation of life's values. We are what we think in our secret place. To observe and register was a most important training in every Indian's life, his book of knowledge.

My storytelling father never forgot. And, when I turn my mind to it, everything he told me is very clear, just as he told me. I can see him as a boy of sixteen racing across the plains, carrying the mail. Dangerous it was, too, with many desperadoes turned loose to kill the Indians for their scalps. I can see him as he roped wild ponies, gentled them to man and branded them with his crossed "J," to start his first herd of horses.

On the great western plains, I see a moving, weaving, billowing sea of grass and sky, swept by the wind across an unlimited horizon, broken only by a group of distant cottonwood trees, telling there could be water there.

It was a lonely life for a cowboy. Under a night star-sprinkled sky I can see him as he sang to a milling herd of restless cattle. His songs and confidence brought them to quietness; they would lie down and rest.

Again I see this boy trying to calm a thirsty herd of cattle seeing a clear mirage across the hot prairie—stampeding to get to the imaginary water. Strange were the stories of the cattle eating the loco weed, becoming wild—fighting and sometimes killing themselves.

Around the herd Father would ride, on his partner, his horse, who understood his talking and singing. He sang to the cattle, he sang to the moon—he made up songs. Hearing his calm, soothing cowboy songs, not only the cattle but all life responded to the rhythm and harmony.

Much modern music seems to be a medley of mismated tunes, throwing the hearers off-balance, inciting violence, arousing morbid passions. If my father had sung such songs around the cattle on the range, there would have been a disastrous stampede—just as now we see stampeding people. They have lost rhythm with the drumbeat of God, who set the timing when he made the world.

Alone on the range a man became very close to his horse, a comradeship unbelievable. A man and his horse became one, his horse accepting the responsibility with the man, learning the cattle and the art of caring for them. The intelligence of a well-trained horse is sometimes uncanny. When I see a would-be cowboy jerking his horse, misusing him in any way, I know he is a phony. There is no rapport. The horse is soon ruined as a mount and hates the man.

My father fell in love with a little filly of racing stock. She was flighty and nervous, having a fear complex—probably from an animal-hating person. He spent time winning her friendship and trust, talking, keeping all his actions gentle and easy. Soon she was following him, nickering for his attention. She blossomed into a fine harness horse with beautiful poise and confidence.

Animals have distinct personalities, just as people do, even the lowest, not one of them the same. Many people go through life missing its very essence, the love of all natural forces and their divine creator. The greatest destroyer of it all is man, the animal of destruction, whose one object in life is to control, to bend to his will every bit of life in his uncontrolled desire to conquer.

My father said: "If you want to know a man, take him hunting. There you will soon know what is inside him—one trip will be the proof." With his respect for all living things, if a hunting companion shot into a covey of sitting quail, or a sitting rabbit, the man was never again asked to be his guest.

When hunting with Father, many is the time I have had a cool drink from a clear stream from the brim of his old Stetson hunting hat, with a bit of dried beef or boiled heart, which he carried in his hunting-jacket pocket. We didn't get hungry, and no messy sandwiches for us!

I have seen first-time visitors to the Indian country stare at the Indians and make comments as though they were looking at animals in a zoo. The Indian pities their ignorance. He shuts out their presence, surrounding himself with a region where their annoying stares cannot penetrate—absolutely aloof. The visitors feel the bleakness and pass on.

Indeed, this is a wonderful philosophy, transmitted down through the generations of time: "Not only ignore by manner the people who annoy you, but learn to ignore in mind. For you they do not exist. You are free." Because of this the Indian has retained his poise and identity down through long-gone-away yesterdays.

Indian children played and had a good time, and were much loved by their parents. They were taught to be most respectful to older people and their parents. I never saw Indian children smacked and pushed around by their parents as white children are. They didn't seem to need it. They knew their place and did what was expected of them. It is all in training. If I asked my mother for a privilege and she said, "No," and if I asked again and heard, "No," I did not ask again. That was it. I did not question. She was my mother.

Now I see some of the Indian children acting like white children, screaming and crying. It seems very sad to me. They are missing so much of this modern world. People are just like everything else—when they lose the rhythm of the drumbeat of God, they are out of timing and lost from the peace and rhythm of life.

Kiowa Sun Dance

Father named me Ho-chee-nee. Sometimes he would call me Chee-nee, but when it was really important, he always called me Ho-chee-nee.

Now I knew this was very important. Father said: "Ho-chee-nee, Chief Lefthand was here today telling me the Kiowas are getting ready for a big Sun Dance over at the old meeting ground on his place on the North Canadian River. The chief wants us all to come, but Mother and I can't go. We have to stay in the store; the Indians will be coming over to trade. The Cheyennes, Arapahoes, Kiowas, and some other Indians are invited.

"This Sun Dance will be the biggest thing in many, many moons since the government banned these ceremonies. There may never be another Sun Dance. We want you to see it, so you can remember and tell us about it. The Sharps are going and you can go with your little friend Bessie."

My, how important I felt! "I am going to a Sun Dance." I thought, "Maybe Mother will let me wear my beaded doeskin ceremonial dress." Mary Lefthand, Chief Lefthand's wife, had made it for me.

This sacred ceremony took place in the spring, about May, as I remember. The cottonwood trees were coming out in their soft gray-green leaves and dripping fluffy cotton that flew lightly and airily on any breeze. The cottonwoods were thick along the banks of the Canadian, as were the willows, which were blooming too.

How I wish I could tell this as it was! These truly sacred meetings with all their tradition and Indian ways are gone forever. They were channels for the inflow of spiritual power, to carry on in the face of the great upheaval that had happened in the lives of these people—their removal to a new country, the destruction of their main source of sustenance, the buffalo. In the hardship of having lost all that was dear to them—for many thousands, even their lives—in their great trouble they turned to the only source they knew, the creator of all life.

Bringing their sacred belongings, the Peace Pipe, the Medicine Bundle, the Tai-me (the sacred doll), all carefully guarded from the old days (as the white man guards his sacred book, the Bible), the people came, hundreds of them, in their horse-drawn covered wagons with the tipi poles tied to the side, wearing their best clothes and ceremonial garments for days of spiritual and physical renewal.

Unlike some Indian dances of today, this Kiowa Sun Dance was not a show performed for the public. There was no "public" there, just Indians. They were their true selves, bringing to life again things of the near past. Indians are not always serious; among themselves they laugh and talk and tell stories, but never their innermost secrets.

The important members of the tribes were assigned special places in the great circle surrounding the Dancing Lodge in the center. It was a thrilling sight to see all those decorated tipis, with important symbols in earth colors, not bright and gaudy as you sometimes see in pictures today but all harmonious as a part of the sky, the earth, and all it contains. They blended in with the color and costumes of the people, Earth People, who once were the masters of this beautiful country, the land of their heart, before they were corralled. This sacred meeting was a reliving and recalling of some of those past days.

Lucky, lucky me, that I could be a part of this picture, even though I was very young. In my memory storehouse it is there, imprinted, unerasable, as part of my early life. How glad I am that I was taught to register. Often I have painted it, from my mind's eye.

The women participated in a most important, impressive ceremony, the selection of the pole, called the "Old Man," which was made of a tree that was tall and straight, with many branches at the top. When it was chosen, a sham battle took place for its "capture." The women cut it down, trimmed off the branches, leaving small parts on to be used as hooks. Triumphantly it was carried to the Dancing Lodge.

There the pole was placed with ceremony in the center, to be used like an altar. Many fetishes were hung on the limb hooks, with other material things and with prayers for help. Around the base were symbols of the hunt and other objects, such as buffalo skulls and prayer sticks.

Many small cottonwood trees were used to make the wall of the lodge. They were planted in the ground to keep the leaves green, woven together with willows, and tied. Forked trees were used to hold up the top, which was made of branches, like a big arbor, with a hole in the center for the pole. One side was left open. It was a very large enclosure, probably sixty feet or so across.

Bessie, my friend, and I wandered around the campgrounds. Several of the main lodges had strings of scalps hanging by the front flap. We thought we would see which one had the most, and I would tell my father. (Speaking of scalps, the Indians were encouraged in the practice of scalping by the Spanish and French colonial governments. Later the United States government placed a bounty on Indian scalps, and the United States Army sold Indian scalps. They were easy to get when they could kill off a few dozen Indians at a time, having got the Indians disarmed and trusting them. Another interesting fact is that sometimes people who lost their scalps in battle lived to tell about it. Probably some of the scalpers got to be quite expert at the sport. They were reaping the reward and found out they did not have to take a life to get it.)

We have read how the Sioux (Little Snake) tribe of the Northwest Plains practiced scarifying themselves during their Sun Dance. They would cut the skin on their chests, loosen it, and then run a strong thong beneath the skin. Tying themselves to the center pole, they would dance until the skin pulled loose and they were released. This was a sacrifice to their religious belief, a mark of bravery. It was horrible. Yet even today we read of religious fanatics mutilating themselves in a frenzy of emotion.

The Kiowa Indians did not practice scarifying. Their Sun Dance was for purification, a test of endurance and power. If blood should accidentally flow, it was a bad omen. The dance would be stopped.

For several days the voluntary dancers had been prepared for the ordeal they were to endure. They said prayers and abstained from certain taboos, such as food and women, and many acts; a married man could not sleep with his wife.

Clearly the years of my memory bring thoughts of long ago. I hear that "beep, beep" of the reed whistle. No man's eye will ever see again this moving, thrilling sight—not a show but a sacred, powerful, mystic ceremony for Indians only. They alone could understand and feel its depth, its meaning.

To the old ones this Sun Dance was living again in the past. They knew the time was near when they would soon take that last journey over the hill. Today they sat, their blankets pulled around them, listening, quietly talking, talking as they called to mind the long past. Their faces were seamed with lines of tragedy, yet with proud resignation, their eyes watery from many campfires. They could tell the story of the American Indian as the Indian alone knew and lived it. Most of their thinking is a closed book to the invading, selfish men who put them away.

Straight and tall, the handsome bronze young men moved around the pole—heads thrown back, their eyes gazing toward the sun, reed whistles in their mouths, with each step of a slow sort of dance, an up-and-down movement. The "beep, beep, beep" of the whistle sounded; on and on it went. The day was warm. Their bare bodies glistened in the sun. On their chests, backs, legs, and arms were carefully painted power symbols: lightning, sun, moon, stars. Around their waists were tied breechclouts, hanging down in front and back. They wore beaded moccasins on their feet.

A young man fell from exhaustion. I thought he was dead. There was no commotion. No one went to him but a medicine man. He squatted down beside him, watching intently. The other dancers danced on as though they did not see. After a long period there would be a short rest, then on again. Four days and nights it lasted without food or water. Some fell out; they could not make it.

It was a distinct honor for any man to be able to finish this purification dance. They had proved they were men, in command of themselves and able to take their place with the leaders of the tribe.

Against the western sky in all its glory, the sand dunes across the river, white against the sky, here in the dancing area, a small flickering fire sending up sweet-smelling smoke, the women were dancing, the Dance of the Corn Mothers.

The throb of the drum echoed against the hills. The men singers chanted the sacred Corn Song, then a gay dancing song. How pretty they looked in their ceremonial dresses: the Kiowas in very full skirts with yards and yards of bright satin ribbon and ribbon falling from their hair; the Cheyennes in their soft doeskin robes, with much bead embroidery; the Arapahoes with costumes much like the Cheyennes'.

The women, mothers of men, represent fertility. They plant the corn, which too, is called the "mother," for all can live on corn. The Sacred Corn was now displayed before the dancing women.

In the fall of the year the finest ear of corn was selected and kept as the Sacred Corn. It must be perfect. It was given into the keeping of a respected member of the tribe. Nothing was allowed to touch it. It was carefully painted green and white and then tied to a prayer stick, reddened with *wase-jido-nika*, or Indian red. The fastening to the prayer stick was made of hair from the head of a buffalo. A single plume from an eagle fluttered from the top of a smaller stick, giving the strength of the eagle to the corn. This was the old way.

Dancing a slow graceful step, black hair shining, ceremonial shawls around them or over their arms, the women in their soft moccasins were keeping time to the traditional Corn Song.

When the song ended, a few grains of the sacred corn were given to each woman to place with her seed corn to make all fertile. A prize of calico, a new blanket, or a shawl was wrapped around the chosen dancer. There was much laughter and fun.

Corn (maize), first cultivated and used by the Indians, is a near-perfect food. It will sustain life in man, bird, or beast. Even fish love corn. When fishing with Father, I would help him bait the fish trap with green corn. We would leave it for a while to soak; when we returned, we would have plenty of fish.

Many years later, while in Alberta Canada, I was invited to attend a Sun Dance given by the Blackfoot Indians. This was a show—a very colorful show, with plenty of blood and thunder. It was performed for a Hollywood movie company. It was not the sacred Kiowa Sun Dance I saw so long ago in Oklahoma.

The Call of the Drum

From the beginning of time there have been Drums—Drums of rhythm—rhythm from the breath of the Divine Being. This the Indian understood and practiced in all his ceremonies, a true expression of the inner man in tune, giving a soul satisfaction and depth to life, profound and lasting, which sustained him in all life's ways.

As the world of the white man closed about him, the Indian's secret dreams were hidden safe within his heart. The white man has never been able to penetrate them, with all his scientific analyses. He is not in tune with the Drums of Divinity.

Thousands of years ago—before the recorded history of man—the folk music of America was created by the Indian. It is still performed today, particularly on the reservations, where it plays a significant role in every Indian's life. There can be no sacred religious ceremonies without the Drum, the rattle, and the ancient, meaningful chants to bring man into harmony with life, teaching patience and respect for all creation.

This oldest traditional musical form in America remains an esoteric mystery. It belongs to the Indians alone, a people trained carefully in a code of conduct and inspiration handed down from generation to generation.

With integration sweeping the world, the younger generation contaminated with modern thought, expressing only the surface man in a most selfish way, the young Indian, like the contemporary white youth, is left without the support of his traditions; all depth of feeling destroyed, he becomes an unhappy, confused, surface-thinking individual, losing contact with his Divine Creator and the drumbeat of life's rhythm. He finds himself struggling in the quagmire of self-pity, off on the wrong road, pushed by television and teachers trained in modern educational technique, without God. We fear these trends will make a nest in the heart of the young and that the soul-satisfying ceremonies will be lost in this spiritless age of speed and misdirected progress.

It requires actual understanding of the soul, its oneness with all creation—every tree, every rock, every bird—to be a complete man, in rhythm with the life cycle of the very earth itself, ancient beliefs, mythology, and natural universal laws.

If you are fortunate enough to attend a real Indian ceremony, listen carefully. Try to remember that you are witnessing a meaningful pageant as old as time. A feeling of awe and wonder will take possession of you, if you are in tune. Hear the throb of the talking Drum, modulated to express the meaning being conveyed, the click, click of the rattle, the tinkle of bells, and that haunting storytelling song. Feel it creep right under your skin—then you are beginning to receive the message.

Many Indians educated in the white man's society—some of whom have become famous—return to die among their people, on or near their reservation home. Only with their own people and the sacred ceremonies that are necessary as breathing, can Indians feel as one with the whole universe.

Dr. Carlos Montezuma, a full-blood member of the Yavapai tribe of western Arizona, became a nationally known physician in Chicago. He was famous for his lectures and books on Indian subjects. In his last illness, tuberculosis, he returned to his people to end his days in the Indian way. He refused to lie in a regular bed, though he could have had any kind of bed he wanted. He chose to rest on a pallet on the earthen floor of the home of a relative on the Fort McDowell Indian

Reservation. Wrapped in his blankets, there he awaited the call of the Great Spirit. His days of fame and glory he put away, to become again —a simple man.

The beloved Oklahoma Cherokee Will Rogers was a regular visitor to his birthplace on his father's ranch, near Collinsville, Oklahoma. There as a boy he practiced being a "roping cowboy," which started him on the road to fame and fortune. Broadway and Hollywood called him to become a celebrity; the world found him. In his natural, lovable way he became known as the greatest wit and philosopher of his age. In 1935 his eventful life was cut short by a plane crash in Alaska, interrupting his dream of returning to Oklahoma to spend his last days in a home built on a beautiful hilltop overlooking the valley and hills of the ranch.

He said, "I never knew a man I didn't like." Everyone who knew him loved him for his gracious, humble simplicity and charm. He was no phony. He was a real, true gentleman—and a Cherokee.

Though he belonged to the world, he came home to sleep, that long last sleep beside his loved ones—on his hilltop dream home—

Where the coyotes howl and the wind still blows free.

Corn Grinding Song

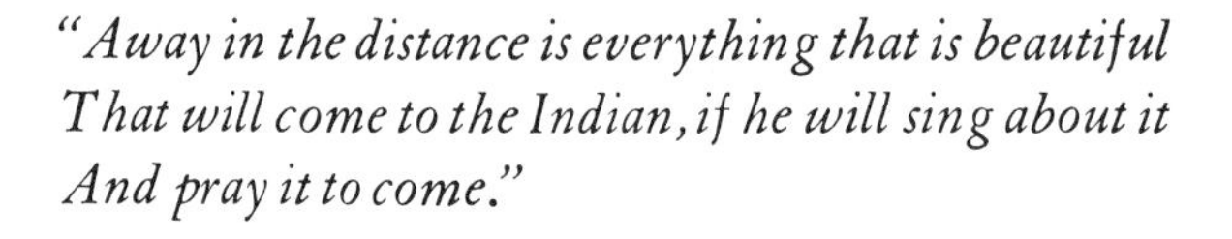
*"Away in the distance is everything that is beautiful
That will come to the Indian, if he will sing about it
And pray it to come."*

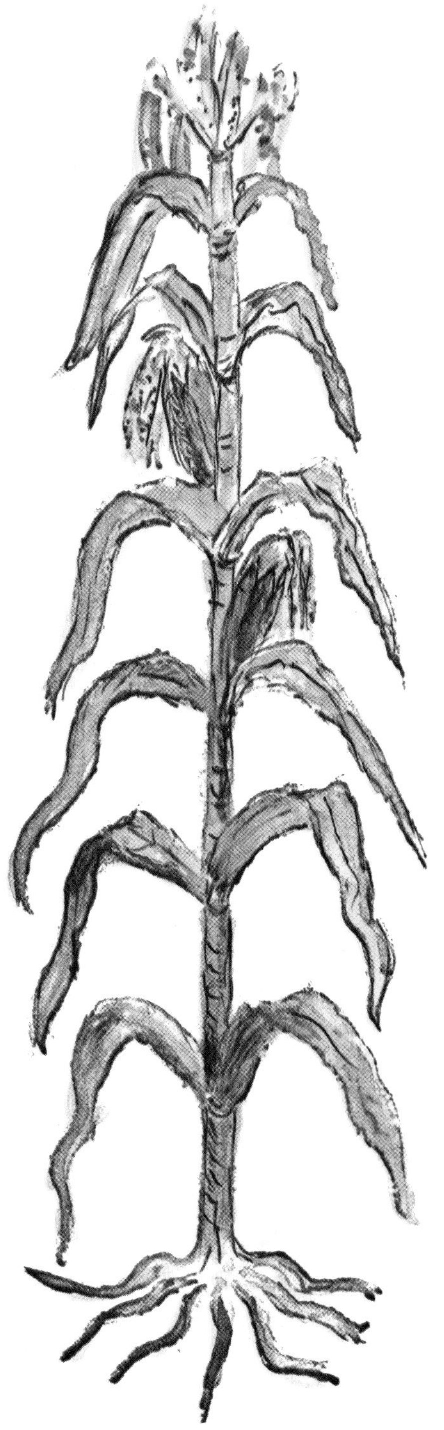

Indian Drums

When the Great Spirit hung his Earth Drum in the center of the blue sky, he placed two great drumsticks, Sun and Moon, to play upon Earth Drum, to bring rhythm and happiness to all Earth children. No man could change his life pattern. Once out of harmony, the world would be no more.

From the beginning there were Drums, beating out world rhythm —the booming, never-failing tide on the beach; the four seasons, gliding smoothly, one from the other; when the birds come, when they go; the bear hibernating for his winter sleep. Unfathomable the why, yet all in perfect time.

Watch the heartbeat in your wrist—a precise pulsing beat of life's Drum—with loss of timing, you are ill.

The Indian was an educated man, a philosopher. He thought deep thoughts, analyzed, wondered, and learned from the open book that nature spread before him. Everything was classified and due its respect for being. The Indian Drum was made that he might talk with the Great Spirit in ceremonies honoring him and carry messages to his people. Every Indian knows the voice of the talking Drum. He listens to the drumbeat of the universe, the drumbeat of God, melancholy and sad; happy and glad; forever it will roll.

As an Indian Thinks

Even today many people, so-called educated people, ask ignorant questions about the First Americans. They imagine that all Indians lived in tipis and wore blankets and feathers in their hair. They would be surprised how often the Indian silently laughs at them, though with pity. But when you remember where they got their information, and that much of the literature about Indians has been written by ignorant white people, most of whom have never even made an effort to understand, you forgive their ignorance. Such writers know more about other peoples of the world than they do about the First Americans.

Now that some writers are more sympathetic to the Indians and realize that there are only about a half million left, they feel a twinge of sympathy and say, "I wish I could do something for the Indians." Others say, "Why worry about the Indians? The government takes care of them." If they only knew. Indians are starving today because the monies collected by the Bureau of Indian Affairs from the Indian reservations and the millions in appropriations from the government are mainly spent in taking care of bureau personnel—not the Indians, who are still tied hand and foot, waiting for government treaties to be honored and make them free men.

The bureau lives high while the Indian lives in a little adobe hut, on the side of a hill where nothing can grow but cactus, while the bureau sends him a nice new garbage can to keep him sanitary. There is a pretty new red-and-blue pump in the yard, but no water. The Indian goes on carrying water for miles. He looks down across the valley. There he sees a white man cultivating a fine, irrigated farm that was once his. The bureau collects the rent; the Indian gets nothing.

The leading officials of the United States government bow and scrape before the heads of godless nations, while the voice of the First American is not heard in the halls of Washington as he pleads for a chance to be a man. More than a hundred and fifty years ago that door was slammed shut. The government had the Indians helpless and starving, at its complete mercy. It has kept them there. The skeletons of tens of thousands of slain Indians rattle in Uncle Sam's secret closet, in this beautiful land of the free.

The Indian is pretty well fed up with the image given him by white writers. He has been called every dirty name in the book and has been the brunt of every kind of vulgar joke. When the soldiers "terminated" them in droves, men, women, and children were stripped, left in vulgar positions in death, showing the sadistic levels white men went to show their hatred.

That has not been so long ago. I saw these things happen through the eyes of the old ones—even my own parents—when I was young. Remember that Indian Territory was opened to white settlement in 1889.

Now and then in movies and TV scripts writers give the Indians a break—let them win a skirmish. They think they have conferred a great honor on the red man. They tell the Indians what to do. They write the scripts to fit their own patterns.

The Indian cannot understand this kind of selfishness. He is descended from ancestors who were not only born free but were taught from birth to respect others' rights, not only those of people but those of all life and the sacred Earth Mother.

They danced, they sang about the hunt and their religious beliefs, and they communed with the Divine for help in all phases of daily life. The philosophy of the Indian was built on different concepts of life's values and his relationship to it all.

The First American

Here is an American Indian—the descendant of an ancient people whose ancestry reaches back to the creation of the world, when God made the red man, giving him dominion over the Americas.

This Indian has withstood cataclysms of flood, the shifting of continents, tenaciously clinging to his Mother Earth. He has been the most scrutinized, analyzed, investigated, tortured, persecuted, hunted, murdered, and finally corralled people in the history of the world. A few managed by the grace of God to survive, to carry on their sacred heritage and traditions.

The Indian is a proud man. He does not want to hide his identity. He has a long and glorious heritage. Scan the histories of time. Read the pages of his achievement. Even though it was often compiled by unsympathetic writers, it is there. Count the food products, the medicines, without which today the world would be in chaos. See the fabulous architectural achievements in Mexico, in Central America, and in South America. Though buried under unknown centuries of time, they remain, the record of a people unequaled.

Look at the paintings of our First Americans in our great museums. There you see men! A proud people, though conquered, they still retain that pride and dignity given them by God, as children of the Great Spirit, and carried in their hearts down through the ages.

Since we know the strategy of the white man in promoting his position all over the world, we can well believe that the "Indian wars" that writers have made much of were financed and waged to assure that the Indians exterminate themselves at the cheapest cost to the promoters. Land the prize. This is the way great conquests were carried out: "Divide and conquer."

The Indians were not a warring people until war was forced upon them by the invaders. Their battles consisted of showing strength and force among tribes. They carried coupsticks. A man who was touched with the stick was out of the skirmish. On his honor he had to quit. Some skirmishes were settled without a death or serious injury.

The jocular, parental attitude taken toward the Indian by some members in our government and the Bureau of Indian Affairs is clearly a reflection of their own mentality. In their surface-thinking brains they cannot conceive of red men being their equal. Well, today there are a few Indians in big business, and their voices are heard. One, for instance, is William Keeler, Principal Chief of the Cherokee Nation. He is chairman of the board of a leading American oil company.

There have been many greats among the Indians of the past. Sequoyah, a self-educated Cherokee, was the only man in world history to invent a written language all alone. Before the Cherokees were driven from North Carolina, practically every Cherokee could read and write his own language. They had become the most literate native people in America, with their own newspaper.

Read the names on statues in stone in the Capitol in Washington, D.C., and scattered over the land. The names of rivers, cities, public monuments—singing names—remind us of a people who left their footprints across America.

In memory I recall one evening when my father returned from a hunting trip to the mysterious Devil's Canyon, in western Oklahoma. Strange stories were told of ghosts and tragedies that occurred in that wild, beautiful place. We were always excited when father came home bringing his game. This night he was not wearing his hunting jacket but carefully carrying it. I thought that he might have an animal, maybe alive. Father said, "Let it alone, Chee-nee." He was telling mother something. He said, "Here it is, Mother." He unrolled the jacket. Then we saw the skeleton. It scared me. I shivered, "Oh, Father, take it away!"

Father said, "Don't be afraid. This is the frame of a man's house. His spirit went to the happy hunting grounds a long time ago. I brought him home to bury; he would like that. I found him on a ledge under an overhanging rock on the high canyon wall."

Mother said, "Maybe you should have left him there."

"But the animals," said Father. "Some of the bones are gone now. We will bury him here. He may be one of the tribesmen who died from smallpox. You remember, when they thought they were going to die, some of them left their families to go off to a place alone and wait for death, so that they would not contaminate the others."

The bones were bleached white from rain and sun. The head was perfect, the teeth flawless. There was no head injury, so the man probably was not shot. Mother and Father wrapped the bones in a sheet and tarpaulin and then buried him on our place so that he would rest in peace.

The sweat lodge was a very important necessity in every Indian settlement. Sometimes each family had its own sweat lodge. It was used often. Some of the chiefs bathed every day when they were at home. They considered it very beneficial to health. A very tight enclosure was built of materials at hand, and placed near fuel and water. Some lodges were ingenious affairs. Stones were heated, and water was poured on them to cause steam. After a sweat period, water was poured over the bathers, or they would go to a nearby stream for a dip. In winter the water was made tepid.

In olden days the Indian woman followed strict hygienic laws. At the time of her purification period the woman lived to herself. She slept alone and ate alone in a lodge. When the period was over, she bathed, using sweet-smelling herbs in her bath (as the men also did in the sweat lodge), purifying herself. She then returned to her regular duties in the family life.

Most Indian families were small, though they willingly adopted children who had lost their parents. The Indians loved and respected their children, who were trained to accept their duties as part of the home and tribe. Rules were strict. The children did not question them. I know that from my own childhood. I knew that my mother loved me, and I wanted her praise. I was never punished. My mother did not believe in training children by force.

Indian babies were kept very clean. They were trained in elimination habits from babyhood, taken from their cradleboards at regular times, taught to obey nature's law. Thus were formed lifelong health habits.

There is no profanity in any Indian language. It never occurred to an Indian to curse anything. Just pointing his finger is enough. I was taught that to point directly at anyone was exceedingly rude.

Osage Homecoming

We are three Indian girls—Mary, Okemah, and I. We are on our way to an Osage Homecoming, honoring two young soldier brothers, home from the United States Army, and their father, a prominent tribesman and chief of the Osage Nation.

A crimson Oklahoma sun is just finishing his day's journey across the great sky tipi, shooting his red arrows to let us know where he has gone. We drive into the grounds surrounding our destination—the sacred meeting place of the Osage Nation for more than a century—the Council House, or "Old Round House," so called because of its circular form.

The Osages are a proud, handsome people. Bravely they defended their homes, their homeland, their way of life, until finally, broken and dispersed, they could fight no more. They were corralled, made to accept some of the poorest land in Oklahoma as their reservation. Fortunately God took pity on them. Oil was found on their land, and the Osage Nation became rich.

Many cars are already in the parking lot near the Old Round House. We smell fry bread cooking. We stop at a stand and sample it with a cup of sofkee, a favorite old-time Indian gruel (I must say that Mother's was much better).

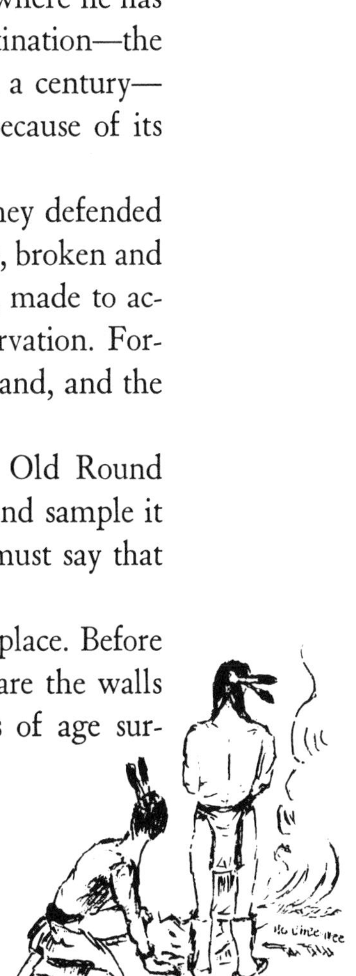

Time turns back as we enter the door of this ancient place. Before us is a scene from a page of a long-long-ago time. Dark are the walls from the smoke of many council fires. The mellowness of age surrounds us. Around the walls are wooden plank seats, tier on tier, leaving an arena in the center with an earthen floor hallowed by the feet of many famous tribesmen of gone-away days, their watching spirit hovering near on this night.

All is quiet; many people are in their places. We see some in ceremonial costumes and lovely shawls, others in regular dress, but with that certain look. You know that they are Indian—they belong.

Mary, Okemah, and I climb upon a seat; we sit, waiting. Here before us is spread a panorama of a way of living that once claimed this entire country. The curtain is lifted; time rolls back. This meaningful, solemn ritual, handed down by a weakening thread of ancient tradition, ties us to prehistoric ancestors that have left mysterious remnants of a vast civilization never yet unraveled.

Seated around the great drum in the center of the arena are eight men wearing the regular costume of singer-drummers—black trousers, Indian shirts of bright-colored sateen bound in contrasting color, western-style hats and silver jewelry, colorful kerchiefs around their necks.

On a raised platform stands the distinguished, handsome old chief with his two soldier-sons in ceremonial dance costume.

A chief tribesman, the master of ceremonies, speaks. He asks prayers for the returned soldiers, for whom this homecoming is being given, and for their father, the chief, who has been very ill. This is followed by a most impressive prayer in the Osage tongue.

The music begins—a soft prayer song goes forth.

With noble dignity the honorees of the homecoming start the march around the arena—first the tall old chief, followed by his two handsome, golden-bronze sons.

The veil of a century is lifted; we feel the presence of those gone-away days creeping over us. The chant of singers and the rhythm of the drums set us in tune. We are living an insistent drama of the long past. This is a serious, prayerful ceremony; we tingle with its sacred mystery. Here, on this very spot, down through the long years, terrible events, decisions, tribulations affecting life-and-death matters were enacted. What stories these dark old smoke-weathered walls could tell. We can almost see the curling gray smoke from the sacred fire drifting toward the smoke hole.

The great drum is modulated as the voices of the singers carry the prayer message to the Great Spirit for the health of this distinguished old chieftain.

Straight like a warrior he is, wearing the traditional formal costume—a fine black Stetson hat, a soft pink silk shirt, its long sleeves gathered into buttoned cuffs. A treasured silver medal rests on his breast. On each side of his navy-blue broadcloth trousers is a narrow satin tape. He wears beautiful beaded moccasins on his feet. With folded arms, in one hand he holds an eagle feather ceremonial fan. Around him, draped over one shoulder, he wears a priceless old-time chief's robe. It is woven of fine wool, in distinct colors, half powder blue, and half a rich red with a two-inch border of the same color. Such robes are rare in our day; most of them are in collections. They were worn only by very important men.

"Tinkle, tinkle," the little bells sound, as the young men in ceremonial dance costumes pass around the arena where the colorful singer-drummers sit around the great drum. The boys are wearing a strange, fascinating roach affixed down the center of their heads that gently nod as they walk along in prayerful attitude (this reminds one: in the long ago the Osage men shaved their heads, leaving a scalplock which was often adorned). A large feather bustle flutters, with smaller circles of feathers on each arm made of many fluffies. Each leg is encircled with long white fur anklets above exquisitely decorated moccasins. One costume is sky-blue, the other gold and black. (Indian people take great pride in their ceremonial costumes. Often many months are spent in their making, along with quite an investment in money. They are carefully cared for, brushed and cleaned after each wearing.)

Now the song changes. The waiting women of the family, standing quietly near, take their place in the procession. Each wears her best dance shawl—often with a long fringe that sways gracefully as she walks. Always the women in a ceremony wear shawls or carry them over the arm. Now they follow the men, as is the Indian custom, their arms folded and heads bowed as in prayer. As the song ends, they return to their places....

Quietly we sit in this humble place, thinking thoughts of the heart. On and on goes the song ritual to destroy evil, to bring health to the sick chief. Reverence completely envelops us. The soft light on the harmonious colors and the evident sincerity of the singers and participants touch the heart and senses—a solemn, faith-inspiring scene. The Old Round House has become a cathedral—we are in the presence of ... God.

The music stops. The moderator-tribesman speaks, "Is there anyone in the audience wishing prayer?"

My friend Mary goes forward. She asks for a prayer song in memory of her father, Chief John Davis, a prominent Creek Indian, who has recently died. The music begins. Slowly Mary, with her gorgeous shawl draped around her, walks prayerfully alone around the arena. We know that she is still grieving for the loss of her father. It is most touching.

Again the moderator speaks: "Our brother and beloved chief, with his two sons, for whom this homecoming is given, wishes to thank every one of you for your prayers and good wishes. He will now speak to you."

Indian character is reticent. It often hides the outward evidence of deep feeling. But as the aged gentleman speaks with quiet dignity, with the distinguished bearing of an old chieftain, tears roll down his coppery cheeks. He thanks his family, friends, and guests for honoring him and his sons with their presence and their prayers for his health. He says: "I feel that I have been made new. Your sincere prayers have touched my body and heart. Thank you. Thank you, every one! Now, to show my appreciation to those who have been with me during my bad time,

I wish to give a special present." This speech he repeats in the Osage language. Then, after a moving prayer of thanks, the moderator again takes over.

The giveaway begins. Names are called. The guests go forward to receive their gifts from the generous pile on the platform. This is a happy occasion of sharing with others, a custom down through the ages. There are fine robes, blankets, heaped-up baskets of food, money. Two white friends of the Osage people, who have lived with them so long that they are accepted as Indians, are honored with a large basket of food. They are the only white people I see at this homecoming.

Long ago in this ancient Osage Council House, many a council fire drifted high, its blue smoke rising to the Great Spirit, calling for his help and protection when human endurance could bear no more. Here the past lives in the present, its strong old foundation and walls having withstood the storms of a century.

The doors of yesterday close as we leave on that moonlit night, still under the spell of talking drum and participation in a ritual of long ago time, a treasure in my storehouse of memories.

We the rightful lords of yore
Are the rightful lords no more;
Like the silver mist we fail.
Like the red leaves in a gale.
Fail, like shadows when the dawning
Waves the bright flag of the morning.

Legend on Antelope Skin

This painting was modeled after those done in early times by the western Indians. Their colors were made from plants and earth. A buffalo bone was used for a brush.

When I was a teen-ager, I saw the sacred Corn Dance shown in this painting at a great Sun Dance that took place on the bank of the Canadian River near our ranch in western Oklahoma.

The central figure is the mythological White Buffalo that brought corn to the Indian, a gift from Wa-Ka-Na-Da, the Great Spirit. The corn was called "Mother," for all could live on corn. The Corn Dance was the most sacred of all ceremonies.

The horses, painted from memory, are riding and hunting horses at our ranch.

In all my paintings I have recorded something from my own life and thinking, as the ancient people did.

The Buffalo

The white rancher of the west regards his cattle as a monetary investment. How different was the attitude of the Indian in regard to his "cattle"—the buffalo.

The Indian thought of this relationship as a fellowship, a brotherhood, each—the Indian and the buffalo—accepting his responsibility as a part of the natural harmony. If the Indian lived according to this plan, the buffalo would come to him. In his ceremonies the Indian gave honor and respect to his "brother," though he would have to slay him.

To the people of the Great Plains the buffalo was regarded as sacred; if it had been sent to him by Wa-Ka-Na-Da, the Great Spirit. It was priceless to him, and its conservation was his chief concern in life (see pages 69, 74, and 77).

Great herds of these animals roamed the western prairie before the coming of the white man. There the grass was rich and plentiful. The Indians' life was good. From the buffalo came their main food, fine skins for clothing, thick fur for beautiful warm robes. The meat was carefully dried to last throughout the year. The buffalo covering for their movable tipis was carefully tanned and sewed together, often painted in storytelling designs. Nothing was wasted. From the horns were made utensils, small cases, dancing paraphernalia; even the hair was woven into rope, and the bones made many useful articles.

Preparations were made for the annual buffalo migration. Prayer rituals were performed with faith that they would bring the herd near.

The Corn Maiden

The Sun, giver of life,
The corn husks and goats,
Corn tassels for fertility,
Evergreen for eternal life;
The corn below,
Rain cloud above,
All mean prosperity
To the Southwest people.

The Corn Maiden

The Fruitage of Corn

In this song ritual the Maize speaks! It is conscious of its mission. It calls to man to behold its upspringing life, its growth, and its fruitage.

In the last stanza its abnegation to man is told, reminding us of man's dependence on natural life. The Indian acknowledged this by giving thanks in his rituals, glorifying the sacrifices made for his benefit by all growing things —vegetation, birds, animals, each one due its special place on Mother Earth, its destiny to fulfill.

This painting was done on a plywood board well covered with glue. Sand was sprinkled over the surface and then carefully pressed into the glue, making a good, smooth surface. The painting was done with caesin and a very dry brush.

Ritual Song

O hasten! Behold
With four roots I stand
Behold Me!

O hasten! Behold
With one leaf I stand
Behold me!

O hasten! Behold
With four leaves I stand
Behold me!

O hasten! Behold
With seven leaves I stand
Behold me!

O hasten! Behold
With one joint I stand
Behold me!

O hasten! Behold
With seven joints I stand
Behold me!

O hasten! Behold
Clothing I stand
Behold me!

O hasten! Behold
With yellow hair I stand
Behold me!

O hasten! Behold
With dark hair I stand
Behold me!

O hasten! Behold
With high, glossy tassel I stand
Behold me!

O hasten! Behold
With fruit possessed I stand
Behold me!

O hasten! Grasp ye,
My fruit as I stand
Pluck me!

O hasten! Roast by a fire
My fruit as I stand,
Even roast me!

O hasten! Rip from my cob
My fruit as I stand
Even eat me!

The dances were thrilling to see. Dressed in ceremonial robes, in pantomime they stalked the great beasts, creeping, hiding, shooting their arrows, while the boom, boom of the drum kept time and the singers chanted their sacred songs. Their prayers were carried out to the Divine Being on the wings of faith.

All this was changed with the invasion of the white man. The Indians must go. The easiest way was to cut off their food supply. Thousands upon thousands of buffaloes were destroyed by "sportsmen" and by bounty hunters. They were butchered in droves. Sometimes only their tongues and hides were taken, to be sold for a few dollars. By the last quarter of the nineteenth century the buffaloes were all but gone. The Indians' food, their way of life, was destroyed. Many tribes perished; driven from place to place, they had no hope. In vain the Indians prayed for the return of the buffalo, for the happy, free days gone forever. Sad were those years, years only the aged ones remember.

No people in the history of the world have been so cruelly persecuted and systematically destroyed. We shudder at the heartless brutality. Ministers in their churches thanked God for the murder of small Indian children, shot down as one would kill game animals, their heads displayed on poles for all to see and glory in. "The only good Indian is a dead Indian." In my own lifetime I have known of terrible crimes committed by white men in authority. Can one blame the older Indians for remembering?

About all that is left of the buffalo ceremony is the fast, exciting dance enjoyed by the young boys. There are not many "straight," or interpretative, dancers left among the tribes.

I will weep for a season,
In bitterness fed
My kindred are gone,
To the hills of the dead.

They died not of hunger
Or lingering decay
The hand of the white man
Hath swept them away.

White Buffalo Dance

In this painting with the buffalo mask, we can visualize the hunters as they pantomime the spearing of the sacred white buffalo hide. Around the fire they dance, chanting and praying for success in the hunt.

The great herds of buffalo that roamed the western prairie were an intrinsic part of Indian life. The buffalo was their food, their clothing, and their homes. The most important date of the year was the hunt. Conservation was practiced for the protection of the herds.

When the white man slaughtered the buffalo, they caused the deaths of many Indians, for without food the Indians were easy prey to the white men's guns. Many tribes perished completely. The survivors were forced into submission.

JIMALEE

The Legend of Creation

In the "way beyond" when the world was new, the Indians lived in the sky as stars. They were very happy there, twinkling, shining, and dancing around the heavens. Many of the lesser stars were birds and animals, which have always been very close to the Indian, even in the sky, and that is why he understands and loves all nature. They were given to him by Wa-Ka-Na-Da, the Great Spirit.

Becoming restless one day, the stars began wondering who they were and for what they had been made. They twinkled over to the sun and said, "O Great Father Sun, why are we here? What can we do?"

The Sun said, "Go to the moon, your mother. Hear her. She knows all things!"

They went trooping over to the Moon. When they asked her their origin, she, with a great sadness, said, "My children, the time has come for you to leave your home in the heavens. You are to people the earth below! Take your little brothers, the birds and animals, with you. They will be your comfort and help. Forever let the radiant Sun be a sign that the Great Spirit watches over you by day and the Moon, your mother, a sign in the night. The stars will be your guide that you may never lose your way. Be true to the Great Spirit. Hold council one with the other and love all living things."

The stars that were to leave the sky dropped down close to the earth. There was no place to stand! It was covered with a great water. They could not return to their former home in the sky. They were very

Legend of Creation—1

In the "way beyond" the Indians lived in the stars. The lesser stars were the animals and birds. The Indians became restless in the heavens. They went to their father Sun asking what to do.

He said, "Go to your Mother Moon. Hear her."

Moon said, "Your time has come to go. Now go to earth, your new home." They did, the animals with them. Water covered the earth.

"There is no place to stand," they wept. The Star People asked Elk, the wisest of the animals, to help. Elk went into the water. He began to sink. He called to the Four Great Winds, "O powerful winds! Come and help me find land for my people!"

They came, East Wind, West Wind, South Wind, North Wind. They blew. The water went up in a great mist, and the Star People had a place to stand. They touched the earth and became people. The lesser stars became animals and birds.

JIMALEE BURTON
HO-CHEENEE

unhappy. They floated around above the earth looking for a god to help them, none could be found. They wept. Remembering what their mother, the Moon, had said, they called a council of stars, animals, and birds to select one to go into the water to find land.

Choosing Duck because he could swim and was a water bird, they said, "Go down, Duck, into the water and find a place to stand!" Duck went down. He swam around and around, looking everywhere for land. At last he became very tired swimming and had to give up. There was no land!

Then they chose Crayfish because he could go under the water. Bravely little Crayfish left his home in the stars and went into the water. Deep under the water he went, sinking so deep that he could not return. He was drowned!

The council then selected Elk from among the animals, since he commanded much respect from all other creatures with his wise and stately appearance. Elk went into the water. He began sinking. Desperately he called, "O powerful winds! Come and help me find land for my people!" With mighty huffing and deep mumbling the winds came.

Until this time there were only two great winds: North Wind, with his icy breath, and gentle South Wind, who was always trying to thaw North Wind and keep him warm. Now the two winds, seeing that Elk was in a desperate situation, said, "Let us make two new winds to help us!" There and then, North Wind and South Wind divided themselves in two, part of South Wind going to the east and part of North Wind going to the west. Thus, East Wind and West Wind were born.

All this time poor Elk was sinking deeper and deeper into the water and calling more and more loudly to the winds for help. Soon the winds came from all quarters with a mighty, crashing blast. They blew against the water with such force that it went up and up in a great white mist. Rocks appeared. The stars touched the rocks and became people. Then land appeared. The little stars touched the earth.

Each took his natural shape and began scampering here and there, looking for food.

When Elk saw all this, he was happy. He was glad that he had been able to help his people, and to express his joy he lay down and rolled over and over (see pages 81 and 84). Wherever a hair dropped from his body, up sprang grass, trees, corn, beans, squash, and everything else that Indians and animals need to eat. They were all very happy.

To the people the birds gave their feathers to keep them warm. The birds also told the people many secrets. Many of the birds—strong Eagle, cunning Crow, fleet Hawk, and Owl (because he was wise and could see in the night)—became the people's messengers, for the birds saw all in their flight.

To the people the animals gladly gave their skins for tipis and clothing and taught them many ways of cunning and thrift, even giving their lives to help the people and make them happy. That is why the Indian has always had much respect and love for nature's children, his little brothers.

The Star People went over the land. In their wanderings they came across footprints that looked like their own. They said, "There must be other people here!" They followed the steps and came to other people like themselves who told them that they were the Water People. They had come from under the water, where they had lived in great shells. Later they met still other people who told them they were the Earth People and had come from their homes in great caverns under the earth.

All these people came together and intermarried, and from them sprang the American Indian.

Legend of Creation—2

The Four Winds blew the water from the earth. The Elk was very happy seeing the Star People on the earth. He lay down and rolled and rolled. Wherever a hair dropped out, up sprang corn, grass, beans, squash—all food for people and animals. Animals gave their skins as coverings for tipis; birds, their feathers. All were content to build a new world. The signs on the tipis symbolize the children of Sun and Moon.

My Family Totem

The hands-and-feet motif signifies the building of the West. The symbol in the center of each hand denotes strength.

The steer skull with the "crossed J" is the brand of my father's ranch.

The man symbol below the skull represents my father; behind him is the store. Below him, the six heads represent members of my family.

The cowboy hats and wampum represent the two cultures of the West.

The Thunderbird is the Indian symbol for the spirit of man, expressing his belief in immortality.

The woman at the bottom is the symbol for my mother. On either side are the two churches she helped build in western Oklahoma. The book and the spiritual eye on each church represent the Bible and the choir—Mother was a singer.

The motif at each side symbolizes the box for the poor, which she kept replenished with her own hands.

My Family Totem

Because of my fifteen-year association with the *Native Voice*, an all-Indian newspaper of British Columbia, and my visits to Canada and Alaska, I became fascinated with the Northwest Coast Indians and their unique art, expressed in the painted carvings which decorate many of their possessions.

The large totem pole was carved only by the tribes of the Northwest Pacific Coast. Once you have seen them, you never forget them. There is power and dignity in each creation: rich and earthy their color, never vivid and gaudy. With a sense of mystery, they seem to be the legendary spirit of the towering mountains and tundra.

Totem poles were never worshiped as idols. They tell, in symbols, the history of the people. The poles, placed in the village, at graves, before the people's houses, represent actual happenings or legends. Their forms were adapted to the poles. The placing of these poles was a festive occasion proclaiming the wealth and prestige of a family. At Juneau, Alaska, I saw several of these poles and was given a small carved pole. I felt very small indeed before these great poles, thinking of the history they represented of a people and a way of life that was satisfying and rewarding. These people were beauty-loving, expressing in their art an advanced culture.

It is a mystery where and when this distinct art of the Northwest Coast Indians began. It was flourishing when the region was first discovered by white explorers. Along the northwest coast of British Co-

The Mythological God of Waters

The mythological God of Waters, carrying sea otters in his hands, with lightning and wind from his mouth drives the killer whale, disturber of waters, bringer of typhoons and destruction to the Northwest Coast Indians. They pray to the god to keep this monster from their shores.

The Eagle and the Killer Whale

On a boat trip up the Inland Waterway from Vancouver, Canada, to Skagway, Alaska, we stopped at Ketchikan, Alaska. It was about ten o'clock at night, but the sun was still shining.

We went to the Ketchikan Museum and saw there a fine collection of artifacts of the Northwest Coast Indians. Among them were several large decorated wooden panels. This painting is decorated much like them. The panels were used as room dividers in the great houses of the Northwest Indians. At a potlatch, or winter festival, they were placed against the walls as decoration.

lumbia and in southern Alaska, on a narrow strip of land with the rain forests and towering mountains behind it, these Indians built their homes and villages. The white men found tens of thousands of them there. The Indians were evidently of a superior intelligence and ingenuity, with a complex social culture. They were well supplied by nature with materials to create luxuries, as well as their needs, and, being an industrious people, they used them all. As woodworkers, they are unequaled in America: as sculptors, they rank with the great artists of the world. Their artistic ability and their love of beauty kept them a very busy people. Moreover, these people were expert navigators. Their tremendous seagoing canoes were up to sixty feet long and could carry many men.

With the coming of the white men, all this was changed. Many Indians succumbed to smallpox and other diseases and to the greed of the invaders. Living on their narrow strip of land, they had no place to go—they died. Today there are only a thousand or so left of these great people. Some of their artistic achievements can be seen in museums; they are treasured relics of a past history to wonder about.

During my studies of the Northwest Indians, their historic poles, and their great houses, I began thinking about carving or painting a totem of my own family's history and its contribution to the building of western Oklahoma. Then, after meeting a world-famous carver at the University of British Columbia, I knew I must do so (see page 85).

Indian Culture

Reservations are lands belonging to the Indian by treaty but held in trust by the Bureau of Indian Affairs. To the Indian tribes the reservations are very important; they are their home base. The people who live there have their own individual culture. People of like culture—religion, customs of living—like to be together; they understand each other.

One cannot tell such people to leave the reservation, forget that they are Indian and be like others ("others," of course, meaning white people), any more than one can transfer an Oriental to the United States and merely tell him to "get along." No matter how well educated he may be in his own culture, if he has no money (as most Indians do not), the Oriental will be completely lost, just as the Indian is. He has lost his base. He is cut off from the tree. For the Indian this is a hard world.

I was once at a fruit stand in Birmingham, Alabama. The Greek proprietor asked, "What nationality are you?"

"I am an Indian," I answered.

"Oh, I knew you were some kind of foreigner!" he said.

When we human beings refuse to look behind the mask of outward behavior to the inner man under the mask, we cut ourselves off from communication. We lose our creative power, and in the end we lose our understanding of all natural life, and even of Mother Earth herself, from which all life's creatures are nourished. The Indian, with true perception in his acceptance of his responsibility to Mother Earth and all she contains, within himself had a sure base in his complete accord with all life. Even to this day he clings to this mystery that supports him. The white man with all his technology and skills and determination has never reached this inner place of refuge and quiet.

In the early days, when favored guests came to call on an Indian household, there were no profuse greetings, questions, or excitement. The guests entered the home in a dignified manner and sat down quietly. Then, after a respectful period the talk began.

The religion of the people was one of harmony. The Divine Creator had given a bit of himself to every living thing, even to inanimate things, such as rocks, earth, water. We speak of living water; indeed, it truly is alive with its life-giving properties. The lightning, the thunder, the wind—each an expression of God's power, setting man back on his heels when he becomes possessed with his own power—are derived from the one source. These forces—moral codes—are as old as man, devised in the beginning when the world was new (page 93).

*The Broken Thunderbird**

The great eagle, beloved by the First Americans, is broken—gone from his ancient nest, just as the Indian people are, before the sweeping avalanche of greed and destruction called "progress." A few sky monarchs still cling to a craggy, diminishing wilderness; the Indian, to a barren, thirsty land called "the reservation."

The Indian revered the Sky King, the eagle, symbol of strength and knowledge and power. He was the master of the air, flying beyond the storm. His piercing eyes brought lightning; his powerful wings, crashing thunder. He brought prosperity in rain to the parched earth.

Eagle feathers were strong medicine, treasured and used in all sacred ceremonies.

The eagle and the Indian still suffer from this ruthless push. Man birds fly their hunting planes overhead, scanning the eagles' last retreat. Their hearts tremble—the Indian's and the eagle's. Will they too fall, to be no more, swept away before this cruel tide of "progress?"

In the blue-sky tipi the Great Spirit watches!

* Originally published in *Defender of Wildlife News*, Spring, 1971.

The Legend of the Kiowa Sun Boy's Medicine

This is a magic story of a time long past, about a beautiful Indian girl and her Sun Boy.

It is said she came to earth singing. The people called her Singing Star. From her former home she brought her own special song about a big, bright, shining star that talked to her and, she said, "watched over her." She was never afraid when Sun went to sleep and Mother Night pulled the dark-blue mystic curtains across the sky tipi. Singing Star was always a leader in the singsong games. Her happy ways made her much loved by everyone.

Now it was the time of the year to gather food nuts for the winter—and such a good time to play in the woods. The leaves had drifted into cozy places to spend the winter—Mother Nature's blanket to keep warm the little animals who were busy making their little nests, where they could cuddle down before the winter clouds sifted gray goosedown over all the land. Even the very smallest of nature's children must have their own homes to feel safe and happy.

In her soft-moccasined feet Singing Star could glide quietly as a falling leaf—not an ear could hear her. She listened to the talk of the animal people and learned many things.

Suddenly a porcupine ran up a tree nearby. She ran after him, thinking that she would like to catch him and get some fine quills to use in the embroidery of her new doeskin dress. Up the tree she went after the porcupine. Magic was the tree, magic was the porcupine. Higher and higher they climbed. With lightning speed the tree grew. Singing Star forgot all but the intense desire to capture the porcupine.

Right through the top of the world the tree grew, into the sky world. In a twinkling the porcupine jumped from the tree. Instantly he was changed into a handsome young man. He was tall and straight, with a princely bearing. His clothes were of the softest of skins. A cloak of brilliant small-bird feathers woven into an exotic pattern fell around him. His hair was long and shining, and he wore a magnificent crown of long plumes on his head.

In all her life Singing Star had never seen a human being so enchantingly beautiful. The young man gently helped her from the tree, telling her that he had seen her playing on earth, had listened many times to her sweet star song, had fallen in love with her, and wanted her in Sky Heaven with him.

Singing Star was completely enchanted. Her dream had come true. When she said, "Yes," Sun Boy placed in her lovely dark hair an eagle plume and carried her to the Moon, who ruled the night.

The Sun was away on his daily journey across the heavens, giving light and warmth to the world below. Sun Boy's mother, Moon, made Singing Star welcome and then dressed her in an exquisite white fringed robe of fine doeskin, embroidered in stardust with red and blue shells that tinkled when she walked. Now she was a real princess.

Sun and Moon called Singing Star "daughter." They were very happy that she had come to live with them in Sky Heaven.

Later, when Singing Star's baby was born, they gave him the important name of his father, Sun Boy. He was a most unusual child. He was not like other children but was born with all knowledge. He went everywhere with his beautiful mother.

Singing Star's handsome husband told her that she could go anywhere in Sky Heaven but that, when she was gathering green foods, never, never to pull the green that had been cropped by a buffalo. She wondered about this. One day when little Sun Boy was with her, she

Kiowa Boy Medicine Legend

The sacred Kiowa Boy Medicine Bundle illustrated in this painting is now in the Thomas Gilcrease Institute of American History and Art, Tulsa, Oklahoma.

I had the thrilling experience of examining and opening it, though the Indian who had been its guardian for twenty-one years said that he had never opened one. He said that he never handled it more often than he had to, on account of its powerful medicine. According to legend, death can befall anyone who touches a medicine bundle carelessly.

My Indian friends were shocked that I should open it. But I prayed in preparation and felt no fear. I was searching for the head of the boy of the legend. I found only an arm. The keeper of the bundle was very old when the museum acquired it and may have removed the head before parting with it.

began thinking about it again. She put Sun Boy down and began digging at a green. The top had been taken by a buffalo. She dug and dug, but the green would not come out. Above her she saw a great eagle flying and called to him for help. The eagle came sailing down from the sky. With one mighty flap of his powerful wings he blew the plant right out of the ground.

Singing Star looked down through the hole that was left, and there she could see the earth below. There was the lodge where she had lived —she could see the smoke coming from the smoke hole. Her memory of home and family returned and with it an intense longing to see her people again.

Spider was nearby working on his web. "Please, Spider, lend me some of your strong silken web," said Singing Star. Spider was glad to help her. Since Singing Star had been taught to weave, as most Indian girls were, with the help of Spider she made a strong rope to which she tied Sun Boy. Then she let him and herself down through the hole in Sky Heaven.

When Singing Star's husband came home and found her gone, he began searching and found the hole. Looking through the hole, he saw his wife and boy slipping away from him down the long silken rope. He was filled with terrible anger. Why would they want to leave him? Quickly he found a big stone. He talked to it: "Stone, go down and hit the woman." "Stone, be careful, do not hit the boy." He dropped the stone through the hole. It sped straight as an arrow to its target. It hit Singing Star, who dropped from the rope and went tumbling over and over to the earth so far below. Beautiful Singing Star was dead.

Natuch the owl, known as the Wise One, saw all this from his home in the big oak tree. He flew to Spider Woman. She was hoeing corn. The owl told her to hurry to Sun Boy, clinging to the rope. Spider Woman knew just how to untie him; then she took him to her home and was good to him. He grew strong and handsome like his father. Everyone was amazed by his great knowledge. One day he saw a gaming wheel hanging in the lodge and asked to play with it. Spider Woman cried, "No, no! I do not want any more children! That wheel will cut you in two." When she left to go to the corn patch, Sun Boy got the wheel and threw it into the air. When it came down it cut him in two. He became twins, with a brother just like him.

The twins became famous. Their lives were devoted to caring for the old ones. They did all kinds of good deeds, even ridding the earth of two great monsters.

One fine day the twins went fishing. Spider Woman liked to have fish with her sofkee, corn bread, and wild greens, and they kept her well supplied. They watched an enormous fish that kept sticking a fin out of the water in the deep hole where they were fishing. The fin seemed to wave at them. Suddenly one of the twins walked into the water and disappeared. The other twin begged him to come back, but he was never seen again. How could the Sun Boy who was left live with half of himself gone? He was so lonely that he sat down and wept. Then to fulfill his destiny he gave himself to the Kiowa people to be forever their sacred Sun-Boy Medicine. Wherever the people went, he would go with them, to lend his knowledge, help, and protection (page 97).

Eagle Feather, the Scout

Black night was silently parting from the edge of the world. Variegated colors crept through the opening where sky seemed to touch Mother Earth. Eagle Feather awakened suddenly. From his eyes sleep did not want to go. Then the old screech owl in the cottonwood tree just outside his father's hogan brought Eagle Feather from his warm bed of buffalo robes. Little Brother Owl was helping open his eyes, as birds do. They have many things to tell, if people will listen.

This was a most important day for Eagle Feather, the day he was to start on a scouting trip to find the great herd of migrating buffaloes for the hunters.

The buffaloes were the Indian's cattle, like the cattle of today. He used them, but he did not lay them waste. He made prayers for them and called them brothers. Prayers, too, he offered, that the grass would be plentiful and green, that all would be prosperous and happy.

For days now the tribe had been talking and dancing, summoning their power for the big hunt so that the buffaloes would come to them.

Into Eagle Feather's mind came a good thought: How proud he was that he had been asked to go on this hunt to find the herd for his people! He was young, but his people had been giving him honor ever since he had found his power, twelve moons past. That was when he had proved that he was a man. Up until that time he had had no real name of his own.

If a boy wants to be a man, there comes a time in his life when he must prove himself, or he remains a boy, depending on others to tell him what to do the rest of his life. This Eagle Feather had been thinking about for a long time. It was easy to see the difference in people who had power and those who did not have it. He thought about his decision to search for power. That was the hard part—but he did it.

He took nothing to eat or drink, only his bow and arrows, a warm buffalo robe, and a pipe with a bit of tobacco to honor the Divine Being. He walked far and then walked more until he came to the place where he wanted to be. There he could see the sun's coming-up rays; that made him feel good. He smoked tobacco to the four corners of the world, then to the sky, then to the earth. He seemed to be praying every time he breathed, all the day long. When dark night crept up to the sky, he could see the stars. The moon was there. Familiar sounds were all around. He was not alone. He went to sleep in his warm robe. He awoke; he prayed for his power to come. He wanted water, he was weary, but he knew what to do. He prayed and slept again.

For four days the sun, stars, and moon came and went, and then from a sleep he awoke. A strong, whispering Wind Voice was pushing hard against him, saying, "Look up, up, up." From high against the sky he could see the wind bringing a tumbling object straight to him. It dropped gently at his feet. He picked it up. It was a beautiful eagle feather. The Wind Voice whispered, "From today you shall be called Eagle Feather. The master of the airways took pity upon you. He has sent one of his feathers, one of the most powerful of symbols, straight from the sky to you. Guard your power well. Never let it leave you. This is your duty."

Eagle Feather felt the warm touch of the Divine Being. Tears ran down his cheeks. A deeply moving sense of perception filled him with happiness. A boy had become a man! He thanked the Divine Being, he thanked the Wind Voice, he thanked the great Eagle.

Eagle Feather's inner hunger had been satisfied; now he must find food for his body. He gathered up his robe and his bow and arrows and went forward to meet the light. This is how Eagle Feather earned his name and gained honor in his tribe.

How Corn Came to the Kiowa Indians

One of the most interesting stories of the Indian's West was the legend of the protective power of the White Buffalo. This albino animal was most rare indeed. Many incidents were told of its appearance when an Indian was near death. Somehow, miraculously, the Indian would be saved. Even white men—trappers, cowboys, and settlers—told of such experiences. This legend was common on the Plains:

Eagle Feather went through the door of his father's tipi. He stopped to take a deep, tingling breath of cool, crisp air. It went darting all through him; that was good. It was the kind of air that makes a man want to do things. This was his day. He felt a deep joy in living. His being sang with a prayer as he went forth with faith. He would find the way of the buffalo for his people. The very life of his people was dependent upon the yearly replenishment of their food supply and upon the fine skins from which they made their clothing and the coverings for their tipis.

Following the path of early light coming up over faraway hills, Eagle Feather went on and on. All around he could hear the little day animals and birds as they scurried about hunting for food. A covey of quail were feeding and talking as they scratched for seed that had dropped with the frost (some animals work at night; others work in the daytime).

Eagle Feather walked silently, with a step as light as that of a fawn.

How Corn Came to the Kiowa Indians

The sacred White Buffalo brought corn to the Indians as a gift from the Great Spirit. This Kiowa legend is told in Chapter 19.

The Legend of the Corn

This sculptured painting portrays the symbolic White Buffalo, bringer of corn. The serpents, symbolizing knowledge, are the messengers of the Rain God. Each serpent bears a month on its head and seven eyes on its body—one for each day. The symbols at each side represent the four winds—the four seasons. The falling rain makes the corn (at the left) grow. The arrows at the right represent man. The sun and the moon represent day and night.

The figures in the painting were cut from heavy cardboard and applied to the base with thick glue. Glue was then applied to the rest of the base, and sand was carefully sifted around the figures, making the design strong and permanent. It was then painted with a dry brush.

He knew the place where the great animals came each year—a place where there was water and where the fine buffalo grass was plentiful. The buffalo grew fat upon this rich grass.

Crossing a low hill, he followed the bench on the other side. Below was the valley. Near the middle he could see a buffalo wallow, a place to which the buffaloes came in the calving season, a large circle where the young were protected from marauding animals by the older members of the herd. There in the center Eagle Feather saw the most magnificent animal he had ever seen or ever hoped to see. It was a pure-white buffalo of great size. With awe and wonder he crept closer to see whether it was real. He raised his bow, but the arrow would not leave the bow. He felt a strange, vague sensation creep over him. He could not move. His legs refused to carry him away. He felt no pain, but he was tied by an unknown power that held him fast.

He prayed, "Divine Mystery, release me from this spell! Give me the answer! Show me the way!"

Then Eagle Feather quietly settled down to await the message.

The White Buffalo stood facing the east. It did not move. All through the daylight time the young man watched and wondered. The mystery held him to the spot; he could not leave. Light went away; the birds quit their singing. Eagle Feather was hungry. From a small buckskin pouch at his side he took some jerky and dried wild grapes. He ate. Pulling his soft buffalo robe around him, he prayed—he slept.

Morning wind brushed Eagle Feather's face. He awoke. His first thought was the White Buffalo. It was still there, but now it was facing west. All day he watched the strange phenomenon. Taking from his quiver the sacred power symbol from the sky, the feather sent by the great Eagle, he talked to it. He felt better. Night came and then another day. At eerie dawn he saw the White Buffalo. Again it had turned, now facing south. The spell held him fast.

Four days the White Buffalo stood, facing east, west, north, south—to the four directions of the earth. Then the White Buffalo was no more.

Eagle Feather's legs were unloosed. He stretched and then went into the valley.

Where the buffalo had stood was growing a tender light-green sprout. Eagle Feather thought, "This must be an omen from the Divine Mystery brought by the White Buffalo." Heaping stones around the sprout to protect it, he started homeward. He must tell the wise men of his people.

While crossing the low hill, his power whispered, "Look beyond the hill!" There before his eyes appeared the herd of buffaloes. On winged feet he flew home to tell the chief people of the tribe where the herd was grazing and to question the hidden meaning of the white buffalo.

There was joy among the people. A guard was placed to keep the sprout from harm. Rains came. Tall grew the sprout, long grew the leaves, the tassel, the ear with hair of yellow-green. Days passed. . . . Brown was the hair of the corn, yellow the long leaves. The wise men talked. The council questioned: "Who will touch? Who will touch?" All had a great fear.

A young man stepped forward. Humbly he said: "For my people I have done nothing. Unimportant is my life. If I die, I will not be missed. Let it be me!" Around the beautiful golden stalk of corn, its long leaves rustling proudly in the breeze, the people gathered. Sacred prayer sticks stood before the medicine man as he chanted a devout prayer to the Divine Mystery for help in this hour of apprehension for the safety of the brave young man who was willing to sacrifice his life to learn for what purpose this strange plant had come to his people. Gently he touched the ear and then pulled back the husk to expose the bright-red grains of the corn. Slowly he tasted, then ate. "Good! Good! Sweet, very good!" (page 104).

A dance was held to celebrate the gift of the corn from the Divine Mystery, brought by the White Buffalo. This was the first Corn Dance. It is still one of the cherished ceremonies of many tribes besides the Kiowa (pages 105 and 109).

The Sacred Corn Dance

Evening comes. The great Giver of Light sinks red. The sacred corn (at the right of the painting), regarded as a mother, sustainer of life, is fastened to a painted prayer stick with buffalo hair, decorated with eagle down. She stands before her keepers. Her tipi is on the left. The women, mothers of men, representing fertility, planters of the corn, dance to the rhythmic beat of the drum and the solemn chant of the singers. Later a few grains of sacred corn are given to each woman to place with her seed corn, making all fertile. Old women, young women dance!

Turquoise Eyes

The first school I attended was a private academy for Indian children. One day as I came home from school, I was thinking, "Why are my eyes turquoise? That is what my teacher said." Most of the children had brown eyes. I asked Father.

He said, "One day when God was making little girls, he had a nice bit of scraps left over. He did not want to waste them, and so he put them all together and made you. God felt rather sorry about you being made of scraps, but he had some extra talents handy. To even things up he gave you one of each kind and said, 'This little girl shall be blessed, and never be lonely.' Now you will have to work very hard to make use of your wonderful gifts."

Mother said, "I was born with rhythm. I was dancing with music before I could walk."

There has always been harmony and rhythm in my soul, an intense desire to get acquainted with and understand all natural life.

A leaf drifts from a tree. I pick it up. How perfectly it is made! I hear a new bird song. A bug does a dance. I wonder. A little animal eyes me from its hole. I sit quietly, listening to nature, thinking, "God must have had a fine time expressing each perfect idea—each its destiny to fulfill. Not a single mistake. My heart feels very big. How can I ever be lonely with all this, this wonderful world (page 113)?

I remember an Indian saying, "Walk lightly in the spring; Mother Earth is pregnant."

How could I be lonely, with the precious gift to be able to create, to make music, to paint pictures, to write poetry, to think, to plan. I did not mind that I was a "bunch of scraps" and that my eyes were turquoise. After all, my father was scraps, too. His ancestors were Indian, English, and Irish.

There is a strange story in the romantic history of my father's paternal family. In that long-ago time soon after America was discovered, there went back to the Old World tales of fabulous wealth to be found in the new country of America. Nations and people were set afire with the hope of conquest and glory.

Among the early settlers in the New World was the Earl of Chetwood, sent by the Crown of England to look after his country's interests. Lady Grace, the earl's young wife, wanted to share this dramatic experience with her husband, but he persuaded her that the hazards would be great and that she must remain in England until he could prepare a suitable home for her.

In those early days it took real pioneers to launch out on unknown seas in small, fragile boats. In some ways the astronauts of today are like them—brave men with vision, eager to explore worlds beyond the earth.

Soon after the earl left England, Lady Grace was told that she was pregnant. Now she had an excuse to go to America. Though she was fearful of being alone on the long voyage, she arranged for passage on the next sailing. She would be with her husband in America for the arrival of their first-born child.

The Peaceful People

This painting represents the home: the bird of peace, the forces of nature—sun, moon, stars, clouds. The crossed arrows symbolize friendship. The bowed arrows mean that, though peaceful, the people are always ready to protect their home.

JIMALEE BURTON
HO-CHEENEE

The voyage was exceedingly rough. And Lady Grace became very ill. Three days before the ship was to dock, she died. There was a law that no one of noble blood could be buried at sea. Her body would have to be brought to shore for burial.

On the morning of the third day the boat docked, and Lady Grace's body was being prepared to be taken ashore. All at once the ship's doctor and his attendant were horrified to hear a deep moan from the body. Suddenly Lady Grace sat up. There she was, very, very much alive!

It was decided that she had been in a cataleptic state—a condition in which consciousness and feeling are completely lost and the body becomes rigid and seemingly lifeless.

Lady Grace recovered completely from her ordeal. She gave birth to a man child, to whom was given the name Thomas. He was the ancestor of my father's family in America. The name Thomas became a family name in the following generations. A Tom Chetwood was a flag-bearer in the Revolutionary War.

Had Lady Grace Chetwood been a commoner and had she been buried at sea, my name would never have been Chetwood (or Chitwood, as it is now spelled)—and my eyes would not have been turquoise.

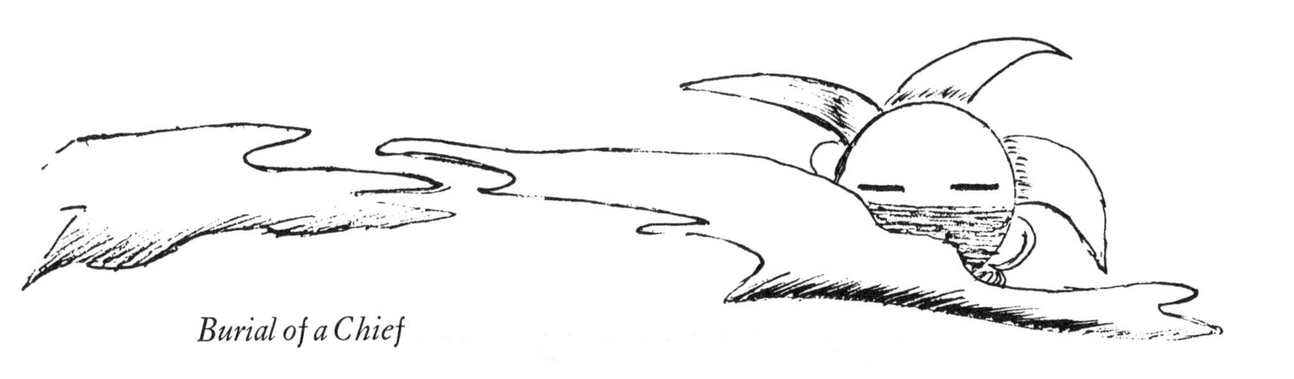

Burial of a Chief

A burial near old Shawnee in Indian Territory before the opening of Oklahoma (page 116):

A day is done, . . . a life is done. . . . The Sun, ruler of the heavens, silently drops into the oblivion of dark-blue night. His parting color arrows, dashing the sky with glory.

In his grave nest the old chief sits alone, in eternal sleep, dropped as a leaf, soon to be lost in the arms of Mother Earth. On the wings of the bird of death his spirit flies beyond the sky, to take its place in the spirit world, where life is ever good—there, where the great peace pipe is. . . .

The last resting place is carefully covered with logs. No earth touches the sleeper. Around him are his ceremonial blankets, hanging nearby is his favorite war shield. At his feet is a basket of food for the long journey. His hand holds a sacred eagle-feather fan for dancing. A headdress of eagle feathers tells of his brave deeds. It has always been worn with pride. Fine moccasins cover his feet. The moccasins are covered with beads, even the soles, since he will nevermore walk the earth.

At the front of the tomb stand his bow and coupstick. The coupstick was used for touching an adversary in a skirmish of strength, not for killing.

This is not a sad place—just a quiet going-away place. To be born—to bloom—to die—is good. Good awaits those whose works have been good.

Burial of a Chief

My mother saw this burial near old Shawnee, in Indian Territory. It is painted as she described it to me (see Chapter 20). She took me to the site when I was very young. The tomb had caved in, the logs rotted or removed.

The painting shows the log-roofed tomb. No earth touches the chief. Around him are his ceremonial blankets; hanging nearby is his favorite war shield. At his feet is a basket of food for the long journey. His hand holds a sacred eagle-feather fan for dancing. A headdress of eagle feathers tells of his brave deeds. His moccasins are covered with beads, even the soles, since he will nevermore walk the earth.

At the front of the tomb stand his bow and coupstick.

Ko-Pi-Sti-Ya
Sacred Navajo Mask

The wearer of a kachina mask becomes the being it represents. Each has its symbols. The turkey tracks on the face represent prosperity; the seeds on the head, fertility; the snake on the horn, knowledge.

These kachina ceremonies were an intrinsic part of the life of the Navajo, reminding him that he lived in the whole universe and making him aware of the psychic harmony. It was his duty to help perpetuate that harmony by his ceremonial life.

The base of this painting is black sand from the lava beach on Maui, Hawaii.

The rituals and ceremonies in regard to death tell of the immortality of the soul. The dying often composed and sang their own last songs. Even dying children did this.

*Last Song**

Alone I am here,
Mother Earth enfolds me.
In her arms soon to be lost.
I have sung my last song.

Above me crying,
The wind ruffles my feathers,
I hear it not.
The sun is warm on my body,
I feel it not.
I have sung my last song.

Alone this house I leave,
No more will it know joy,
No more will it know sorrow,
I have sung my last song.

* Originally published in *Arizona Highways.*

Burial Customs

A monument dealer tells of the erection of a beautiful granite stone for a prominent Indian family at an old burying ground in the Cherokee Nation. An aged matriarch, the last of her generation, died, leaving orders that her best clothing and personal belongings should be placed in her tomb. Her son, a college graduate, attorney, and a progressive leader of his tribe, ordered her wishes to be carried out in strict secrecy on account of the danger of vandalism.

A large waterproof box was built of reinforced concrete to act as the base of the monument. Inside this base were placed several new, expensive suitcases filled with many exquisite handmade shawls, ceremonial costumes of beaded doeskin, eagle-feather fans, bolts of finest silks and satins, Indian jewelry, personal treasures worth many thousands of dollars, fine rugs, and other items that should have been in museums.

Everything was tightly sealed, and over the base was placed a mammoth pink-granite stone, burying priceless treasures from sight forever.

From the time my memory began, hidden in my consciousness was a horror of being in a tight, confining place. I shrank from the thought of dying, because I had seen dead people placed in deep holes in the ground and earth piled on top of them. It worried me. Probably other children have had the same feeling about death. But this was before I heard some aged Indians talking about ancient burial customs. I listened, and what they said was good. Their description of the Indian tree burial calmed my fears.

They told how after death the body was carefully prepared and then dressed in its ceremonial garments for that last long sleep. The face was painted in the old symbolic way. Friends and relatives came with their mourning songs and prayers. A medicine man performed the sacred rites. While chanting prayers for the departed, he sprinkled sacred cornmeal, called the Mother, over the body (the cornmeal was used like the holy water of Christian churches). Then, brushing the face and hands with a ceremonial eagle feather, he transferred the touch to each member of the family, "for remembrance."

The traditional arrow was shot to the place where the sun goes to sleep, symbolizing the spirit taking flight into that unknown, faraway place beyond the sky, there happily to await its loved ones from the earth.

The body was wrapped in soft blankets, and a large animal skin was laced around it. Then the body was gently placed high on a scaffold built in a large tree or on a frame of four poles about six feet above the ground. Leather thongs bound it there, making it safe. Day would come; night would come—Mother Nature always there to watch and care for her own.

I thought, "Death is not a bad thing; what the old people say is good." Just like a tree house—always I had wanted a tree house (I built one for my cat, Boy-Cat, and he loved it). That was for me; no more would I be afraid.

To myself I said: "High in my safe nest, there with the four winds I will rock. The sun will shine warm on me. I will not mind the rain. When night creeps down over the great sky tipi, the moon will light my tree house. The Milky Way will make a glory path for my spirit.

"Day will bring my gentle little redbird—and Mr. Dove with the broken leg that Mother put in splints and healed. They will bring their friends to sing for me, while Sala-li, the gray squirrel with the talking tail, will bark and scold."

Never, never, to be alone. That was not like dying at all; it did not even make me sad. I will not be put in the ground in a tight place. I will

The Great Spirit speaks
In wind voices,
In rain fingers
In the eagle's flight
Many the feathers in war bonnet,
My brave deeds known.
I go beyond the place of thunder;
Like the eagle beyond the lightning.
I fly beyond the sky.
My eyes to the east,
My heart in peace,
I fly beyond the sky.

*I Fly Beyond the Sky**

The Indian believed in the faraway place of long abiding. There the spirit would go to be at peace, surrounded by all the things of his dreams of happiness. In this painting the spirit of man, bearing the earth symbol on his head, rises from the earth to fly beyond the sky, carried by the sacred Eagle Spirit.

* Originally published in *Arizona Highways*.

be free with the wind and the rain, safe in the arms of our Mother Nature, while my spirit on the wings of the arrow sails on like the powerful eagle to explore the unknown mystery we all wonder about (Plate 21).

My earth body will be left to mingle again with the earth as a leaf lost in a gale. My wish will always be that I might be buried in a "tree house"—a beautiful place for a last long sleep. Those days are gone forever, but I will never forget the "tree house."

The Mexican Boy Who Became an Indian

"Come on, José, hurry!" shouted Andrés Martínez. "Hear those old goats a-bleatin'? They're hungry! They want to get out of that corral to eat. Tela and Padre are through milking. Padre is going to Las Vegas today.

"If you want to go to the desert with me, come on! We'll have fun! Maybe we can catch a rabbit. I have my flint, and we can make a little fire and cook him on those rocks we fixed.

"Tela has made us a good dinner—some frijoles, tortillas, sweet peppers, and *azúcar terciado* (brown sugar), too!"

Doña, the sheep dog, was wagging her tail and waiting in the doorway, where a first streak of morning sun was peeping in. Doña knew that she was a very important dog. Every day she took care of the sheep and the milk goats and these Mexican boys, Andrés and José. Doña knew just what to do. She understood the animals. They trusted her. So did the boys. Andrés knew the words his mother, Tela, had taught him to command Doña. She had trained Doña with the herd.

José finally got his sandals fastened and his little serape over his head. He took a tortilla off the table, rolled it around a piece of mutton, fixed another, put it in his pocket for Doña, and then followed Andrés out the door of the low adobe house.

José was just five years old. His cousin, Andrés, was a big boy and pretty smart, too, for seven years old. José and his pretty mother, Cosetta, had lived with the Martínez family ever since his father went away.

Andrés opened the corral gate. With Doña behind them, pushing and sometimes leading, the animals rushed out and down the path, Andrés and José trotting along behind. Today they would keep the herd near home. Padre was away, but they were not afraid with Doña with them. They always found things to play with. Today it was a little horned toad. It really looked more like a short lizard than a toad. It was such a cute little fellow. To watch it snatch ants and bugs with its long tongue was exciting to the boys. When José held it in his hand, it would flatten out, and it seemed to like having its little horny head rubbed, if José was very gentle. The boys never kept a toad for long. They had to eat—lots of bugs.

The boys were eating their lunch when they saw a party of Indians come riding toward them. Andrés had heard his father say that the Mescalero Apaches had been raiding not far from there. They had taken horses and had killed some sheep, which they had carried away with them. Andrés was plenty scared now. He and little José crawled behind some mesquite bushes, hardly breathing.

The Indians knew that there had to be someone close by. People do not leave sheep and goats to wander around the desert alone. They began riding around, looking. They found the boys and pulled them out. How the boys kicked and fought! But they did not have a chance. The Indians carried the boys to their horses and tied each of them behind the saddle of a rider so that they could not get away or fall off.

The Indians sometimes stole children and sold them, or kept them to replace ones they had lost. The Mexicans did the same thing. It became customary after the many wars, the displacement of the people, and the great loss of life.

The Indians got on their horses and hurriedly left with the children. All day they traveled. At night they made camp, built a little fire, and gave the children some jerky and sofkee. José would not eat. He was sick and cried and coughed. Andrés was too scared to say anything. But he ate all he could, still hoping to get away.

The Indians did not like José crying. They tried to hush him and make him feel better, but he would not stop. Andrés was so tired that he went to sleep. The Indians awakened him early the next morning to eat so that they could be on their way. Andrés looked for José. He was gone. The Indians said that they had sent him home, but Andrés believed that they had killed him because he was sick and cried. Andrés was very sad but afraid to cry.

As the Indians traveled on, they met a party of Kiowas on a raid looking for horses. They said that their horses had been stolen by some white soldiers. One of the Kiowas, Set-dayu-ite (Many Beans) liked Andrés and bought him. He could not understand the name Andrés and so called him An-deli.

Before long An-deli began to like this man as he rode along with him. By the time they arrived at the Kiowa village in Indian Territory, they were good friends. Set-dayu-ite gave An-deli to his wife. They had lost their son, who had been killed by Mexican raiders. She was glad to have An-deli and adopted him as her own son.

It was customary that, when a war party took a captive, anyone who had lost a child could adopt the captive. After an important ceremony the adopted one became a full member of the tribe, in all respects as one born so; he was subject to the duties and requirements of the family by a kind of new birth received in an impressive ceremony before an ensemble of the chief people. A chief made a small cut and then washed away the blood, symbolizing the severing of all connections with the past. The adopted one's new birth was confirmed and sanctified by the smoking of the sacred pipe. He was then named and dressed in new clothing befitting his new name and place in life. After the ceremony all the participants were served a big feast.

An-deli was a smart boy. He grew to love his new family. They were good to him, and he soon forgot his past. Years later, on a visit to a store in Anadarko, Indian Territory, the headquarters of the Kiowas, he saw people getting letters at the post office. He remembered

—and asked the postmaster about the letters. When asked his name, he had a hard time bringing it back to mind. Then it came to him. He said, "Andrés Martínez, Las Vegas." The postmaster sent a letter to Las Vegas, New Mexico. A reply came back telling of the abduction of the children many years before.

The Martínezes were overjoyed that he had been found and wanted him to come home. An-deli was also excited, but he could not leave his Kiowa parents, who treated him as a much-loved son.

An-deli became a recognized leader and interpreter of the Kiowas, speaking fluent English, as well as Indian languages and Spanish. On trips to Washington to see the Great White Father, An-deli served as the interpreter.

A Methodist missionary who was helping my family organize a church brought with him as a volunteer An-deli, the Kiowa Indian. He told my parents the story of his life and how he became an Indian. Later An-deli married the daughter of the missionary. They worked with him in his mission work in early Oklahoma.

Looking through a copy of the *Annual Report* of the Bureau of American Ethnology for 1895–96, I came across a picture of Andrés Martínez with the caption "Interpreter, and leading man of the Kiowas." I remembered this story, told by An-deli to my people, who related it to me when I was a child.

Religion in the Territory

Billy Sunday, the famous turn-of-the-century evangelist, made many trips to Indian Territory.

I met him once on a train. My father was taking me on a trip to Memphis, Tennessee. Billy Sunday got on the crowded train. My father recognized him and asked him to sit with us. We shared with him the box lunch Mother had packed for us.

One of Oklahoma's most interesting Indians was the Osage chief Star-That-Travels (better known as Bacon Rind), of Pawhuska, capital of the Osage Nation. He was a great admirer of Billy Sunday. Among his treasures were photographs taken of Billy and himself (they are now in the Oklahoma Historical Society Museum in Oklahoma City).

Bacon Rind was one of the few remaining full-blood Osages to cling to old Indian customs in dress, as well as other matters. He was an outstanding figure in his glossy otter-skin crown cap, which added stature and dignity to his bearing. In March, 1932, he passed on to the Happy Hunting Ground, dressed in his choice Indian garments, and was buried at noon, as the sun was sending down its perpendicular rays, the time when the spirit may pass through the heavenly gate.

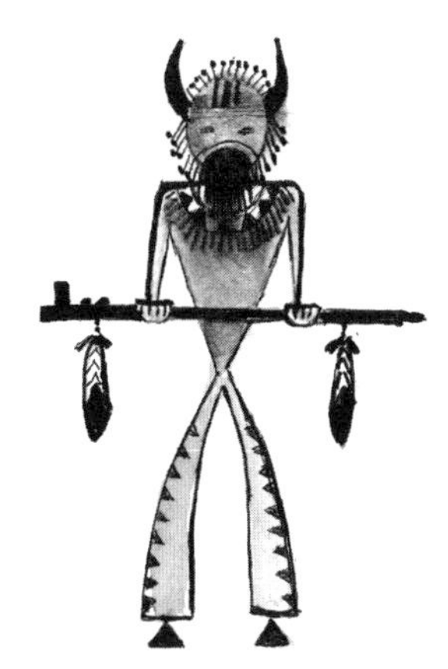

Buffalo Dance

Night and Day

This painting is modeled after Navajo religious sand paintings. The figures represent night and day. On the black figure (night) are the moon and the constellations. On the blue figure (day) are the symbols for corn, beans, squash, and tobacco.

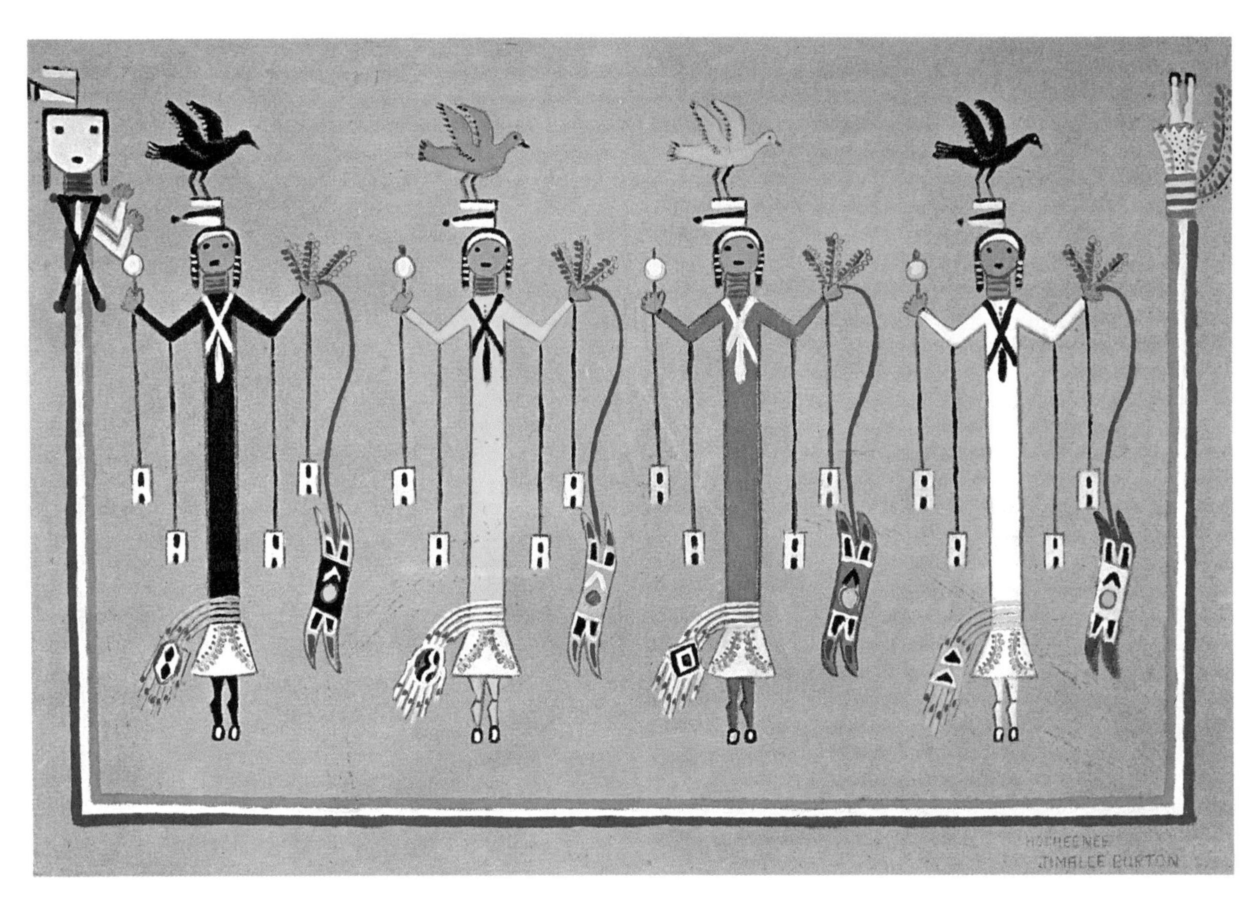

The Four Seasons

These figures represent the four seasons and fertility. The birds on the heads are protectors, as is the rainbow goddess surrounding the design.

*This Is Where the Indian Got His Sand Paintings**

Wind I love—rain I love—
I love the surging sea.
I vibrate to the pulsing earth,
Which is a part of me.

Pure and white the sand I touch,
I know in every grain
Is part of a forgotten form
That may take shape again.

The blue sky tipi overhead,
The unfathomed, changeless sea—
God paints his pictures on the clouds
For all, a gift that's free.

* Originally published in the *Sarasota Herald Tribune*, May, 1971.

Sand Painting

Fanciful forms of a fantastic dream world can be seen in drifting clouds. Watching them can be a soul-cleansing experience. Should we question what ancient mythology tells us: "The mystic Sand Paintings of the Navajo Indians were first shown to them on clouds and yellow fog"? Just as biblical prophets received instruction from the heavens, so did the ancestors of the red man.

These paintings, executed by medicine men, are used as prayer messages to God for help in dire need or the healing of those who are ill. According to legend, night must never fall across a sand painting. As the Sun finishes his day's work bringing light to the world, the sand is gathered up and cast to the four winds as part of the sacred ceremony.

The paints are made from colored rock, carefully ground to powder. Black is obtained from a tree burned by lightning. The color is poured slowly on a sand base to form a religious mosaic. There may be several helpers if it is to be a large painting. It has no power unless it is made strictly according to ritual (pages 128 and 129).

A lifetime of devotion to studying and memorizing each detail of the long ceremony is a sacrificial work.

BURTON
JIMALEE

The Sun Dragon

In the sun there is a dragon,
His tongue is hot and red,
"Be careful, do not trust him,"
The Indian mother said.
"He burns the corn,
Curls the grass,
The throat of beast is dry.
Great Spirit, give us rain
Or we will surely die."
All painting nature seeks to hide
From his stinging dart,
Seeking out each living thing
To stop its beating heart.

Ho-Chee-nee

The Mystic Ginaly-li, My True Friend

A long, long time ago a first-American artist carved from stone the small, strange buffalo that I now treasure. When I hold it in my hand and feel its surface, worn smooth by the hands of a people long gone to the spirit world, I look in its deep turquoise eyes and wish it could give to me the ancient stories of its journeys—the tragic days, the happy days my little buffalo has seen with a people to whom it represented a way of life for eons of time. Now that the buffalo is gone, these legends with their profound ceremonies belong to the ages, in forgotten history. Only a smattering told in the white man's uncomprehending writings remain.

This carving was given me by a mystic medicine man, who placed his age at many, many moons—near one hundred, I was told. Yet he was straight and tall, with that certain Indian dignity and reserve that comes from within, often misunderstood as unfriendliness or resentment. On his wise old weathered face was etched a story of time, a picture from the past. Under his black Stetson hat with its narrow band of tiny beads and a small feather at the side one could see his black hair, plaited in the old way with red and yellow yarn. From his little home on a hillside where he farmed a small patch of corn, each day he came—swinging along with an ageless step—not plodding as we might say of the old ones—three miles to town, to sit a while and then return home again.

I would see him come and would hurry over to his shady resting place to sit with him. I listened all ears as he talked. Mother had taught me about herbs and healing power. Ginaly-li taught me more. With deep, spiritual sincerity he talked of his medicine, his power, and his search for magic potions to bring healing to his people. When he told me special things, I was honored. Mystics do not often tell their secrets—learned from a lifetime of study.

Many word pictures he made for me of tribal ceremonies of long ago—to guide the wayward to the straight path. From his heart, thinking carefully, he would talk—then talk no more. Sitting there with his blanket pulled around him, Ginaly-li seemed to gaze through the shadows of today into a time far off in memory. In his way he was so calm, so poised, that I sensed the deep knowledge behind his half-closed dark eyes and felt that he could look straight into my soul. Yet he was so kind that I felt good, with much gratitude for the privilege of sitting with him and possibly sharing his dreams of long-passed days about which I wanted so much to know.

Ginaly-li said: "This is a white man's world. He talk, talk, talk. He say words off the top of his head—they mean nothing. He no think, he can't stop. He want, he get. He has no heart. Never satisfied. Yet he has no more than me. Only one life today—tomorrow he die."

"Have patience," he said. "All things change in due time. Wishing cannot bring autumn glory nor cause winter to cease."

He said: "There is no fear where there is faith—to walk the straight road with the Divine Being, to feel his quiet whispers of beauty in your heart."

The following is what he told me of an old-time buffalo ceremony in which the ancient small buffalo fetish that he had given me was used. It was a religious meeting for the renewal of faith and trust. The participants in this ceremony were all from a special society.

Around the wall of a large lodge were placed couches, each covered with a blanket. The floor of the lodge was of earth, packed hard and smooth as concrete (the same kind of floor can be seen in Mexican churches, smoothed carefully by the hands of devout women using water and clay). On the floor were scattered rugs.

On the hearth below the smoke hole in the center of the lodge was a small fire of glowing embers. A thin wisp of smoke curled upward.

Now the people came, wearing their ceremonial dress of soft Indian colors—their hands and moccasins stained with red earth. As he entered, each participant was given a rawhide rattle and was assigned a place, the men on one side of the lodge, the women on the other. A chief served as master of ceremonies and the keeper of the sacred buffalo medicine bundle containing mystic medicine.

From the fire the chief took red-hot coals one by one, piling them before him on the earthen floor where he sat. On them he carefully sprinkled sweet-smelling herbs from a small pouch at his side. As the smoke rose, the aroma of the soothing, pungent scent drifted over. The ceremony began.

Like a sighing wind, deep and low, the voices of men and women mingled in sonorous tones—a song without words, keeping time to the rhythmic "click, click" of the rattles.

Now the chief in a clear tenor voice sang alone, while taking from its leather wrapping an image of a buffalo carved in stone. Seven of these small bundles were spread out, each in its own case, and a special prayer song was sung. The song had been handed down through time; no one knew its beginnings.

During the buffalo period of the American Indian's life these rituals could go on for hours—yes, even days, when the people felt a great need. They were always conducted with reverence for the buffalo and recognition of the brotherhood of all life, created by the Divine One for the good of all, with prayers for the knowledge he had given us to know.

When the ceremony ended, each member was given a symbolic mark on the forehead with red tint and wishes for good luck and peace.

As the people went out into the night to return home, they felt a closeness with the Infinite—the union of heaven and earth and all it contains. Life was good—they had been blessed—their thought temples cleansed and refreshed.

Spirit of Silence

Teach me, O great spirit of silence,
To find thy presence on the altar
of inward peace.
In deep love and joy to vibrate with
The eternal mystery of creation.
To behold you in every life expression.
To feel you there, in every beat of my heart.
Through the depth of meditation,
I receive thy supreme light—
O thou glorious Spirit of Silence.

The Song of the Windmill

A thirsty, rainless summer day. An erratic wind blows across the land. The windmill quivers and whirs. She almost stops; then another gust of wind, and on she goes with her job of pumping. You breathe a sigh of thankfulness. She is there; the wind still blows. The West was built with the windmill and the wind.

No man has ever devised a better or cheaper way to raise water from Mother Earth. Fortunes have been made from fine cattle fed on bluestem grass and good water. Our friend the windmill is the heroine of it all—with her affinity, the wind.

In the great open spaces of the West there had to be water for man and beast, or today there would be no West as we know it. What music could be sweeter to the ears of the rancher than the song of the wind in the windmill? How well the cattle, too, know that creaking and swishing of the windmill shaft as it drives deep to an underground stream to bring up sparkling-clear, cold water—the very essence of all life. The cattle will drink and be satisfied.

Ominous is a silent windmill under a cloudless sky with no wind to sing in the wheel. All hands must take a turn at the pump to put water into the tank. Or the cattle will tell you of your neglect. Across the grasslands one sees these wonderful windmills spotted here and there—the great fan wheel with its weather vane pointing the way of the wind, clear, cold water pouring into the big tank, thirsty cattle coming to drink. Even the birds and the wild beasts seek this man-made

oasis. Somehow it seems a part of the landscape, a nostalgic symbol of home.

City water is something to quench thirst, but a cup of pure, cold water from Mother Earth's refrigerator is the nectar of the gods.

The windmill at our house on the ranch had a screened cooling shed attached to the pumphouse. As the water came from deep down in the earth in a long pipe, it was released into a covered trough. There we kept our milk and butter in heavy crockery jars. Many a juicy melon floated there. It was a most efficient refrigerator. We had ice only when someone made the long trip to town. Then out came the hand-cranked ice-cream freezer. The pumphouse was a lovely cool place on a hot summer day. That was where the ice cream was made. My sister, Maudelia, and I were always there, ready to lick the paddle when it was taken from the freezer.

One day my little cat, Billywink, and I were watching some sun perch swimming where the water ran into the big tank. They had been put there by Father. The thought came to me, "Can Billywink swim?" To find out, I suddenly pushed him into the tank. My, what a horrible yowl he gave! I was scared, too. His eyes! I'll never forget his eyes as he looked at me when I helped him out. Poor little cat, poor me! I cried. I prayed to be forgiven. I think that was the meanest thing I ever did.

When I am in the cow country and see the windmills and the cattle standing around, all these memories return. How I would love to live those years again, close to Mother Nature: breathe that good, sweet earth smell, see the cattle around the haystacks in the winter, ride my pony across the ranch with Father, hear his old hunting horn and the yelping of the hounds as they follow the trail, listen again to the song of the windmill, watch the sparkling water gushing into the tank, see the eagerly drinking cattle—become one again with God's country.

The West was built with a masterpiece, the heroic windmill and the wind.

An Indian-Summer Day

This was an Indian-summer day, when all the old Indian spirits return to visit the earth. The soft haze and the smoky smell in the air are their pipes with their sweet-smelling tobacco. Happy is he who can catch a glimpse of these old Indian spirits dancing, dancing while they sing of the good old days—the good old days when Mother Earth was their home, with all her bounty their very own.

Indian summer is a magic time to wander in the country alone, to explore the mysteries of nature, to think with eyes that see, to shake off the man-made touch of every day, to become as one with the unfathomable all and feel its closeness around you. It brings a soul renewal for a few hours.

On just such a day with my husband, Dan, I went on a short trip to an oil lease east of Tulsa, near Collinsville. While Dan was talking with the driller, I looked for something to occupy my time. In a big pasture I saw several horses and mules. Horses are my love, as well as all other animals, both wild and domestic—maybe I was an animal in my last incarnation. I crawled through the barbed-wire fence, taking some apples with me, hoping to find some friends.

There had been a light frost, just enough to show where a cold finger had touched the vegetation—it was the miraculous, glowing, changing time of the year.

The broomweed stood leafless, straight and sturdy, its top covered with gold. Broomweed was mother's favorite remedy for a cold. She made a tea of it; it was "burny," like pepper, we said.

The scrubby blackjack oaks were bright in their special red. Every kind of grass had received new color, its very own. What greater magic could we find than this? I found some devil's-claw, a short-lived, spectacular, orange-flowering annual with a curved, giant claw and lacy texture. The dried flowers are sometimes found in souvenir shops. Breaking open a pod, I ate some of the seeds, just as we used to do when we were children. They are good, rich and nutty. A friend once told me that the Indians used the plant for making dye.

I started out to get acquainted with the horses—but wait! Here is a tall, spiny plant, its pods bursting with downy little umbrellas to which are fastened tiny seeds. I touch one—off it sails on the wind, nature's way of spreading her species, and a soft, warm lining for bird nests.

A little burrow is at my feet. Stopping, I wonder about the animal that might live there. I am careful not to disturb it, remembering that each little fellow is born with a right to its own niche in the great plan. Just because he is not my kind is no reason that I should dislike him. According to Indian teaching, he is our little brother. We, being men, must respect the divine law.

Well, I am coming closer to the horses. I begin making my funny get-acquainted song to gain their attention, to let them know I am a friend. They come toward me, ears pricked up, listening. I hold out my hand, talking softly. I call this my horse talk—just for us alone. The

lead horse comes first. He sees the apple and carefully samples it. I scratch his head. Then they all want to see. I am having a wonderful time. With good friends like this I never once think of being afraid. I am sorry when Dan calls me to "come—let's go."

On the way home Dan tells me how shocked the driller was when he saw me in the pasture among the horses. "My God! They will kill her. Those are wild horses! The only way I can catch them is to run them down and lasso them." Dan told him, "Maybe you don't know horse talk. I never worry about her among animals. She understands them—especially horses."

This was a beautiful Indian-summer day to remember and share with you. A way to find happiness in little things. On such a day when there is a smoky smell in the air and a misty haze hangs over the land, do look carefully. When you see a glowing spot of color on leaf or grass, this could be where some old, tired dancing Indian spirit sat down to rest, leaving some of his red dancing paint. If you are in tune, listen! You may hear a soft hum, as they talk of valorous deeds of Earth Days, long, long ago!

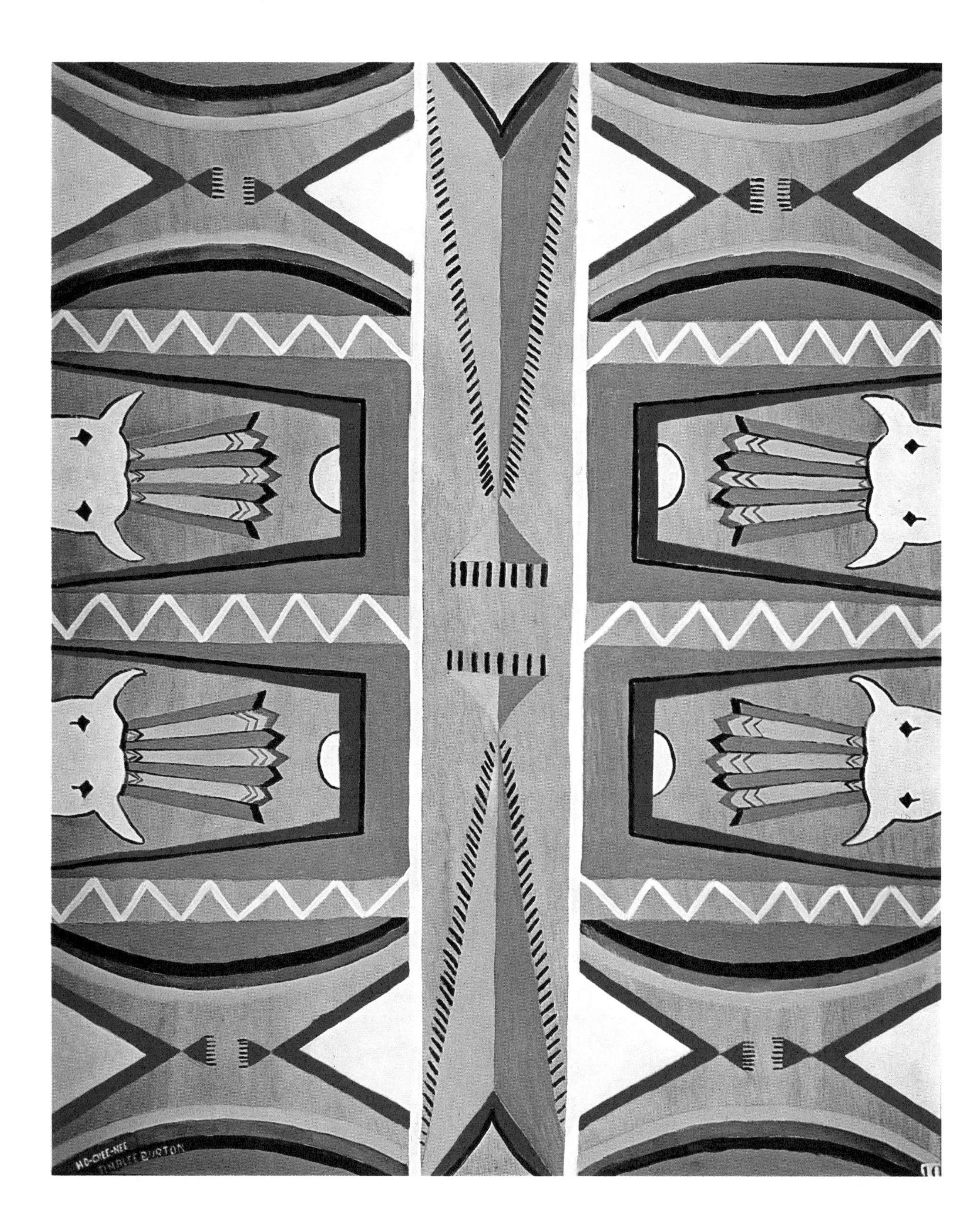
HO-CHEE-NEE
BURTON

Sac and Fox Parflèche

This painting, modeled from a Sac and Fox parflèche, shows the tipi symbol, in a meadow with a lake. The buffalo symbols and the zigzag trails denote the presence of many buffalo. The painting, on a wooden panel, was made with a dry brush.

Parflèche

The Plains Indians knew the buffalo and gave him honor in their decorations. Many of their possessions carried symbols representing birds, flowers, and animals woven into fascinating color and design (pages 144 and 148). The colors were made from pulverized rock and earth and sometimes the roots of plants. Natural colors were permanent. Parflèches were used as storage boxes, trunks, carrying cases. They were made of strong rawhide, prepared in a special way so that they could be shaped and laced together. Beside each bed in every well-furnished tipi would be a parflèche in which personal possessions were kept.

Arapaho Parflèche

In this painting the tipi symbol appears at each side at the bottom. At the bottom center is a hogan surrounded by a corral. In the center on each side appears the bird of wisdom and strength. Yellow represents the shining sun.

Into Silence the Indian Went

Into silence the American Indian went for purification. Schooled in the ways of nature, with deep understanding in his heart, he found power in the unseen force round about. The Voice of Silence speaks a universal language, a voice for every listening ear.

Seeking the answer for the stress of life's problems, alone, with fasting and prayer for the purification of mind and body, he found peace, whether in the waving billows of a golden-grass sea, on a western plain, in the rustle of dry cottonwood leaves, or in the chant of high-sailing geese—a divine guidance is there. It is a part of the profound mystery, the drumbeat of God.

While thinking deep, long thoughts—vibrating with sincerity and integrity—becoming as one with all nature—a soul-satisfying peace came to him. There is no translation for the Voice of Silence; its purification is in the heart alone. The renewing life force penetrates the whole being.

The man straightened up. He breathed new life; he was a new man. Perhaps a new name came to him from his experience.

Rejoining his people, he perhaps gave a special ceremonial dance, he the actor and dancer, telling in pantomime and story of the intensely felt change he experienced—the thoughts he had while on his communication watch (pages 153, 156, and 160).

These purification journeys sometimes lasted for days, without food or water. The time was spent in close communication with nature and the Great Spirit. It was a severe test of power and self-mastery, a sacrifice made that he might receive a longed-for blessing.

Through complete abjection and self-denial he was released from thought burdens and purified. These rituals, taught by the mystics, have been the sustaining force of the American Indian through long years of persecution and sorrow. Through them he remains an Indian.

Purification

A Storytelling Dance

Seeking the answer to life's problems, the Indian went alone into silence. By fasting and deep communion with natural laws, a reaching out to the all-powerful Mystery for help, thinking deep thoughts, vibrating with integrity and sincerity, a soul-satisfying peace would come. By purification of mind and body he found the place where peace is. In this painting he is telling of this great experience in song and dance, in an impressive ceremony for his friends.

Smallpox Time

Just as a mother cat or wolf will carry a sick kitten or pup away from the nest to protect the well ones, to let it die alone, or as a wounded buffalo leaves the herd to die in some wash on the plains, so the people of the reservations and the Indian villages followed the natural law—the tribe must not be endangered. The sick would creep away from camp into the woods or high grasses, there to die alone.

The mother of the late Maisie Hurley, my dear friend and editor of the *Native Voice*, of Vancouver, British Columbia, was an early-day missionary to the Canadian Indians. On a trip in the back country she saw an aged Indian woman, who, knowing she was nearing life's end, had crept away to a lonely place to await the call of the Great Spirit. From memory she recorded the singularly tragic scene. The painting is now in the Museum of the Indian in Vancouver.

Thunderbirds weeping

Overcoming Evil

Overcoming Evil

This man is facing life's problems.
Donning his ceremonial costume,
With fasting and prayer,
Guided by the star of soul wisdom,
He takes his restless, disturbed mind,
Into the deep silence of meditation,
There to commune with the Divine
Ruler of all life.
Man cannot circumvent this rough road.
He must go over it, to put it behind.
He shakes the rattle and tomahawk.
His power helping him,
Great courage comes.
Again he is brave.
He is satisfied.

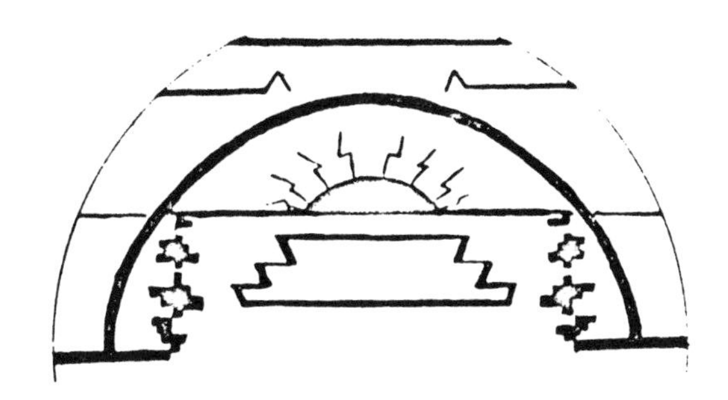

Ceremonies

The words of an Indian song recalled an incident, a story, or a personal emotion which the song commemorated. For this reason it is difficult to translate the words for an English-speaking reader, and it is almost impossible to communicate the meaning and the dignity of the words.

The American Indians sang about everything that affected their lives. Sometimes a person, through prayer or a moment of stress, received his own special song. Only he was allowed to sing it. That right was sacred.

America's oldest traditional musical form still remains an esoteric mystery. It has not been contaminated in the ceremonies observed today. It is a sacred and profound element in the life of the descendants of the First Americans trained in the tradition of their people. The music, the rhythm have a depth of meaning that scientific analysis has never been able to penetrate. It requires the understanding of the soul, and the complete man, according to Indian conception. It comes from his innermost being, connecting his everyday life with ancient mythology and beliefs.

The dance is a channel not only for the outlet of aesthetic nature but also for the inflow of spiritual power. From ancient times the people have sung in times of trouble and danger, to cure the sick, to confound their enemies. They have sung to make the crops grow. Song was their most precious possession. The words were filled with good; they softened the heart.

Prayer Altar

With prayerful faith in the great spirit, symbols are placed on the sacred altar for consecration.

Each symbol in the painting represents a thing hoped for: Clouds bring rain—rain means that corn will grow. The green willow means prosperity. The serpent is the underground messenger to the rain gods. The prayer stick with eagle down symbolizes strength; the circle, unity of the people. The feather headdress is a blessing for the owner.

Indian Music and Dance

The Greeks danced in their temples; David danced before the Ark. The Indian, the First American, danced as an offering to the supernatural being who gave to him Mother Earth and who taught him oneness with all nature and his dependence on universal harmony.

To this day these dances and songs are preserved and enacted during special ceremonies, ancient rituals as old as the mind of man—a very necessary, basic expression of reverence for all life—unveiled for his own soul satisfaction and self-realization, bringing close harmony with the cosmic universe and man, the supreme masterpiece—dancing before his Maker.

Around the great drum in the center of the dance circle sit the drummer-singers, each holding a drumstick. There can be six or more, according to the size of the drum. Over each dancer's dark trousers he wears a soft shirt of silk or sateen, bound in a contrasting color. Around his neck is a colorful kerchief held in place with a silver slide. He wears a broad-brimmed Stetson hat encircled with a narrow band of beads or leather. At the side of the hat is a small feather. Around his waist is a concho belt of silver.

Nearby sit four women, selected for their fine voices. They wear colorful shawls woven in the traditional patterns, with deep fringes. Around them are their treasured ceremonial shawls. Silver and turquoise jewelry shine. They are the choir.

The drum vibrates. . . . A clear tenor voice starts the song. Circling come the vivid feather-bedecked dancers, silently taking their place for the sacred introduction of the dance. There is a feeling of reverence and wonder as the voices of the singers rise and fall with the perfect rhythm of the throbbing drum. Though one may not understand the words, yet he knows that this is a fervent supplication to the Divine One for all the wants of mankind.

Now the dance begins. The dancers present an actual scene, telling the story in strict time. They dance to the wail of the wolf—the lonely pleading of the loon—the night bird's call—the pantomiming of the buffalo hunt—the all-pervading, all-comforting hum of nature told in a song story of heroic deeds and legends to be remembered.

The onlooker who fails to see in the measured step and the constant repetition of syllables something beyond modern music and dance misses the mysterious, profound meaning of the whole performance. At first you wonder—but wait. Sit quietly, and you, too, will soon be vibrating with the pulsing beat of the drum. Now the ear catches the melody that reveals the intent of the strange drama, so full of color, movement, and meaning. The dance is short. It stops—as one with the beat of the drum.

Some ceremonies, such as the sacred Corn Dance, Rain Dance, and Night Chant, have many songs. Any mistake in ritual might bring disaster. All tribes have their own important dances.

Having heard some Indians speak in broken English, few white people are aware of the fluency, force, and beauty of expression of the languages of the different tribes. During the time of the resettlement of the Indians in the West, many of the chiefs visited Washington, D.C., to plead for the safety of their people. The government officers were confounded by the fluency of their speech and their gracious manner. Often when the speeches were translated there was no English word or phrase to express the same thought. Many of these famous speeches were recorded and can now be read. Though the English translations are inadequate, they give the reader some hint of the beauty of the originals.

Those who live and have their being in harmony with natural law, realizing the divinity of themselves and of all creation, naturally express themselves from their understanding of self and spirit. The haunting cadence of the Indian song is the rhythm of the universe and the im-

mensity of space, keeping alive the memory of valorous deeds, stimulating a heroic spirit among the people.

Songs, like the language, were transmitted from one generation to another, strict care being taken to preserve accurately both song and language—no liberties were permitted with either. Songs were property: they belonged to a society, to a gens, to an individual. If a song belonged to a person, he alone could sing it unless he gave permission to other singers. There were songs for all occasions, even death songs.

One story from the page of Indian history tells of the death of a loyal chief who tried to protect his people when they were driven from their homes by invading settlers and government forces. The chief, standing straight and tall with his face turned toward the heavens, stood dedicating himself to the Great Spirit, while in a clear tenor voice, which had probably led many a sacred ceremony for his people, he began his death song.

Again and again the soldiers fired. Still the chief stood. They became frightened before this mystery of strength and fortitude, and cried out, "Can't we kill the old devil?"

While singing, a man was not concerned with his audience. He was not seeking to present a musical picture—his mental attitude was wholly subjective. He was completely occupied with voicing his own emotions; consequently, he generally paid little attention to shading or expression—but rhythm he always had. This is a marked characteristic of Indian music. Everything in all the universe moves and has its being in complete rhythm; so has music. If rhythm is broken, that is the end.

Man, animals, the earth, the sky, and all natural phenomena are not only filled with breath but bear a relationship one to another different from that which the average person is accustomed to consider as existing among them. Man does not stand apart. If he is in tune, he becomes literally a part of Mother Nature, connected to her physically and related to her psychically.

Hear the hum of wind through great trees, the katydid song, the traveling song of high-flying wild geese, the dripping of rain on cool moss—all in perfect rhythm. This rhythm the Indian understood and practiced in all his ways. The pages of nature were his book of knowledge. His songs and dance, his rituals all attest to this profound fact.

My mother loved to sing. She was constantly organizing singing groups. Poetry, the church, and music were her main joys. She never forgot a song. She could entertain us any time with her poetry and songs. Her wish was to be able to sing the clear, bell-like tones her father had taught her.

Mother would often tell us of her schooldays at a Quaker mission in the Potawatomi country in Indian Territory (Mother called it "Pot Country"). There she was given her first Bible, which is now in the Oklahoma Historical Society Museum.

In that mission Indian songs were discouraged, but in the early evening when night came down and the stars hung low across the valley and the hills near the mission, the children would go to their favorite sing-place. Dividing into two groups, they would go to a hillside rendezvous. There they would chant their ancient spirit songs to each other across the valley. As the sound echoed on and on from the hills, the valley was filled with voices—"spirit voices" my mother said—singing with the children.

How enchantingly beautiful it must have been, there alone with Mother Nature, each small singer expressing his soul's harmony, with joy and happiness. Around them their little animal brothers kept watch from the darkness. The children, the spirits—singing under the great night tipi dotted with stars.

To the Indian, dance and music with their profound ceremonies were life in balance, expressed in the throb of the drum, modulated by the singer-drummers, the voices synchronizing with vibration of the drum. Every emotional feeling could be expressed then, with faith given over to the Great Spirit for his consideration and help.

These sacred ceremonies with their many songs of gratitude and supplication, performed by the medicine man, the chiefs, and leading people of the tribe, sustained and strengthened the people morally and physically when they were in dire need, especially after the upheaval of their lifeways after the coming of the white man.

To these early invaders and their missionaries, Indian ceremonial music and dance—and all their ways—were so foreign to anything they had known—that they saw the Indian as nothing less than a "barbaric heathen." With only themselves forming a pattern from which to judge, how could they understand? Their natural instinct was to change, eliminate, or appropriate for themselves everything they wanted. Reason ran riot when they saw this bountiful America. They would conquer, they would take it, and they did. Yet with them they carried the Bible!

Had ancient biblical doors of the past been open to them, down through the gallery of time they would have seen great biblical characters, such as David, expressing every emotion—heartbreak, joy and elation, oneness with God, the animals, birds, Mother Earth, the waters, lightning, winds—even the smallest of the creeping things.

In David's divine, inspired poetic music he sang, he danced—offering a beautiful paean to his God that has been sung on down through the ages. This we know: the Indian, in his great tribulations, was reaching to the Great Spirit for the same wisdom and mercies as had the great and beloved David, with a song for the heart and not for the ears alone.

The wavy lines represent the sound reaching the head or body, not the ears.

The Indian's Gifts to the World

An old Cherokee Indian legend tells that diseases and medicines originated thus:

At one time the birds, the beasts, and the plants could talk. They came together, declaring war on man because he was killing with the bow and arrow without asking permission. First the bear, then the deer, and then the other animals took a vow to avenge themselves. The plants would not take the vow. They declared that they would supply the remedies to heal man—they would not enlist in the cause of death.

That, says Cherokee myth, was the beginning of medicine and of how the medicine man found his power to mix roots, barks, leaves, and seeds. The medicine man also believed that the waters have great curative powers in the autumn. The leaves of trees and certain herbs mingled in the water have special medicinal value as a poultice. The autumn is also the season of the Medicine Dance.

The American Indian contributed untold gifts to medicine and also to man's food and sustenance. A few of his gifts are tobacco and rubber. Tobacco, originally used for ceremonial purposes, has been abused by man to his own detriment. The discovery of rubber gave man mobility and an untold number of products.

Probably the American Indian's most important contributions have been food. We seldom stop to think what would happen if all the foods discovered and cultivated by the Indian disappeared from our dinner tables. To lose just one item—corn—would be a calamity. Then there are cacao, from which cocoa is produced, and white and sweet potatoes (the "Irish" potato is not Irish but Indian—early explorers took it back to Ireland, where it thrived and was later returned to the Americas as the "Irish potato"). Tomatoes, squash, and many kinds of fruits and nuts—including the peanut—were first cultivated by the American Indian.

Probably the Indian's most useful gift of food was corn (maize). In Peru I saw many many kinds of corn. One variety had kernels as large as one's thumbnail. Many of our foods—among them corn—were first cultivated in Peru in the stupendous hanging gardens on the sides of the Andes Mountains, watered by snowfed springs and irrigated by sluiceways. Luther Burbank said that it took those patient gardeners hundreds of years to produce corn. The Andean gardeners were a hard-working people—they did not spend all their time in religious ceremonies and pageantry as some scholars would have us believe.

The American Indian contributed more to man's culture than food and medicine. He was a master architect. It took a thorough knowledge of the principles of engineering to construct the great buildings, with their beauty and power; to cover them with graceful, intricate carvings; to fill them with paintings and sculpture that, though buried for many centuries, still remain to thrill the imagination, to cause wonder and admiration in any viewer. Their structures were practical as well as beautiful. Today in Mexico City an aqueduct built by the Aztecs is still in use.

The early Indians were skilled in the surgical arts. In the Inca Museum in Lima, I was shown evidences of surgery that had been performed on human beings hundreds of years ago. The skeletons, which had been well preserved in dry cavern burial places, bore evidence of leg and arm fractures set in such a way that they had healed straight and strong. Several skulls had been operated on successfully. The miracle is that such operations were performed with obsidian knives.

The ancient Incas were not only skilled surgeons but also master weavers. The clothing worn by the skeletons was extremely finely woven. The director of the museum showed me a piece of cloth one inch square containing over 500 stitches (today machine-woven cloth of 190 stitches is considered fine weaving).

Although the Aztec Indians of Mexico far excelled both the ancient Egyptians and the Babylonians in their knowledge of the heavenly bodies—the movements of the sun, moon, and planets—their master achievement was their calendrical system, exact to the day. They discovered a system of measuring time in fixed periods and of dating events accurately in their order of occurrence, using numbers in a way that indicated their grasp of abstract mathematical quantities, including zero. It was one of the outstanding achievements of man. While I was a student of art in Mexico, I saw the famous Aztec calendrical stone.

Indians of the Northern Hemisphere also contributed to the intellectual development of man. The famous Cherokee Indian Sequoyah was the only man in the history of the world to invent a written language alone and unaided. The Cherokees called it the "talking leaves." They mastered the writing very quickly, and soon nearly every member of the tribe could read and write. The first Cherokee language press was established at New Echota, Georgia. When the Cherokees were driven from their homes and businesses in Georgia and North Carolina and forced to move to Indian Territory, they were the most literate group of Indian peoples in America. They had advanced rapidly in education and living standards; many of their children were sent to England to be educated. For their efforts they were forced to make the horrible trip over the "Trail of Tears" to Indian Territory. The Cherokees lost more than a third of their people along the way. Among the dead were the wife and child of their beloved chief, John Rogers. A cultured, educated people —herded like animals. But that is another story.

The Indians of both hemispheres excelled in handcrafts. They were outstanding basket weavers, using the materials they had at hand. I have seen small baskets made of tiny bird feathers—so finely woven that one can hardly see the weaving.

As ceramists the Indians had no equals. Their creations are light and airy, showing no mark of a mold. Modern-day ceramists are confounded, unable to explain how the Indians developed the craft into such an art.

María Martínez, of San Ildefonso Pueblo, together with her late husband, Julián Martínez, also a noted artist, brought back to life a long-lost art when they created their famous black-on-black Pueblo pottery. María has been honored by presidents, a king, and a pope. María of San Ildefonso is a famous name among collectors all over the world.

There are many famous names in the records of the American Indian. Among them are Charles Curtis, a Kansa (Kaw) Indian, who was Vice-President of the United States under President Herbert Hoover; N. B. Johnson, a Cherokee and a justice of the Oklahoma Supreme Court; and the present Principal Chief of the Cherokees, W. W. Keeler, president of Phillips Petroleum Company. A man whose record has never been equalled in the sports world was the Sac and Fox Indian Jim Thorpe, of Carlisle Indian School, a winner in the Olympic Games in 1912. He died of a broken heart—his medals stripped from him through jealousy.

It would take a book of many pages to tell of all the contributions made by the American Indian to the world. I have mentioned only a few in these pages.

A Cherokee Martyr

The following version of the death of the Cherokee martyr Tsali was told to me by a friend in North Carolina, Sarah Beck, editor of the *Cherokee Times*.

A man named Tsali (or Charley) was taken in a roundup of families for the removal of the Cherokee Indians from Georgia to the West. Charley, his wife, his brother, three sons, a daughter, and their families left together. As they were being driven along the road to the stockade, Tsali's wife, who had been sick, was not able to keep up. The soldiers prodded her along with a bayonet to hasten her steps. When she fell, it was more than Tsali could bear. He persuaded his comrades to join him in a dash for liberty at the first opportunity.

The move was sudden and unexpected by the soldiers. One soldier was killed, and the rest fled, leaving their charges to escape to freedom. A hundred or more others, some from the stockade, made good their escape to the mountains, where they hid out, subsisting on roots and wild berries until the hunt was over.

General Winfield Scott, finding it impossible to capture the fugitives, agreed to leave them alone, provided they would surrender Tsali and his party for punishment.

On hearing this, Charley voluntarily came in with his two older sons and his brother, offering himself a sacrifice for his people.

This hero, his sons, and his brother were shot near the mouth of the Tuckasegee River, in North Carolina. To impress the Indians, Cherokee prisoners were compelled to be the executioners of their brothers. From these few people and another group who fled into the mountains arose the present Eastern Band of Cherokees in North Carolina.

Mr. Charley

This is to introduce you to Mr. Charley, my father's favorite hunting horse. Mr. Charley was a really handsome horse, with unusual markings on his sleek dappled-gray coat. He is shown in the painting on the antelope skin (page 69), with my pony, Pompey, and my sister's pony, Billie.

Mr. Charley was affectionate and gentle. He loved people, because we loved him. He knew it. Horses are like the people with whom they associate. If you meet a bad horse or a bad dog, "you can bet your bottom dollar," as my father would say, "that animal has had a bad experience with man."

When following the hounds in a chase, Mr. Charley was plenty fast. A rail fence meant nothing to him; he sailed over as though it weren't there. He was one smart horse and pretty proud of his accomplishments, as was Father! Charley was not gun-shy, but Father was careful never to shoot over his head. He had respect for Charley. They were pals.

That Charley was clever about figuring out gates. He would fool around with one, and pretty soon out he would come for a stroll. One day Mother was watching him. She saw him open the gate and told Maudelia to put him back in the corral. He had on a halter and a short rope. Mr. Charley wasn't willing and didn't want to be bothered. Maudelia was just a little girl. He didn't have to mind her. As she reached for the rope, Mr. Charley caught her by her long braided hair and lifted her right off the ground. Maudelia screamed. Charley dropped her and stood looking down at her, pleased with himself. Mother said, "He turned back his lip and actually laughed."

Maudelia wasn't hurt. "It was so funny," Mother said, "that finally she laughed too."

One hot summer day Mr. Charley came limping in from the pasture. Father and I hurried out to see what was wrong. Father said, "Let me see, Charley." That horse actually lifted a foreleg. We could see that he had a bad snag just above the knee. We immediately started treatment with arnica and bandages, but a fly had already got to it. Father said, "Now, Ho-chee-nee, you have a new patient." I am a natural "medicine doctor" anyway, always taking care of some bird or animal, like my mother. She knew the herbs, barks—about everything good for healing. Charley was a fine patient and most appreciative and cooperative. He would stand without flinching when I treated him with the antiseptic, which I knew burned terribly. Mr. Charley was one smart horse. The wound healed quickly, and soon Charley was well again with only a little scar.

Mr. Charley, the horse, Dick, the pointer, and Father were three great pals. They understood each other. They had perfect rapport. It was a joy to see them together. When I could tag along, that was even better.

When Father came out of the house wearing his hunting jacket, his gun on his arm, Dick went into action, yipping and prancing as they went to the corral to get Charley. The breath-renewing touch of fall was in the air, with a soft, hazy crispness—just the kind of day to put mystery and wonderment into the heart of a woodsman, who is tied to all nature. The crunchy drying grass—the cattle all fat and content. None of the other ranch dogs went on these trips; Father liked to watch Dick work alone. What a picture to remember when Dick would freeze on a point!

The Black Rag was Dick's registered name at the kennel where father bought him when he was on a buying trip in Kansas City. Father loved dogs, and he had to have the best. He trained his bird dogs himself. They learned to work together.

One of the first things Dick did after he came to live at our house was chew up a fine leather seat cushion that belonged to Mother's little buggy. Was she mad! But Dick soon outgrew those baby ways, when he learned about birds, guns, and hunting. Dick was a born hunter.

Dick's attitude toward the other ranch dogs was most superior. He was proud; he alone could do the bird hunting. A real personality he was—just the way he walked proved he was quality.

Dick slept in the house in a special bed under Father's big old roll-top desk. When the hunting season was over, he was always at the store. That proved to be bad, for he made friends easily. With his handsome, sleek, all-black coat, with a few pure white hairs making a formal tie at his throat, he was admired by everyone, especially the hunters. He became a champion, and hunters wanted to buy him, but a dog like the Black Rag you just don't sell. They are part of the outfit; they have to be there.

But a calamity happened: Dick disappeared—gone. Father thought of suspicious characters he had seen around the store. He put out a search. On a trip to El Reno, Oklahoma, by train, while walking down the station platform, he looked in the baggage coach—there was Dick!

He called, "Dick, Dick, is that you?"

"Yip! yip! this is me!" Dick was as excited as Father!

In a big hurry Father hopped into that coach and cut the leash, and off they went, pronto!

Charley and everyone at the ranch were glad to have Dick home. Dick, a great pointer, Mr. Charley, a sweet horse, and Father—three good pals.

May the winds of heaven blow softly on all who share your heart and wigwam.

*My Prayer**

O God, give me a loving heart and an understanding mind—Teach me to be submissive as Christ taught us to be—

Let me know the workings of nature and man that I may better cope with daily life—

In my home let me always be ready to do what is asked of me, if it does not interfere with Thy plan, that I may promote peace, happiness, and tranquillity.

Keep ever before me this—He who loves best serves or sacrifices most—

Keep me from ever complaining. Remind me there may be those who do not feel as well as I—

Give me sympathy and understanding at all times, and always give me the right words to soothe the rising storm clouds of everyday life—

Let me always have a soft answer and words of praise—

Show me the beauties of life, and let me find happiness in little things—

And above all, let me be thankful for what I have, and am, and expect to be.

* Originally published in *Psychology Magazine.* Soon after this prayer was first published, I was stopped by a traffic officer on the street. "I want to thank you for this prayer," he said, and he pulled it from his pocket. "You will never know how it has helped me." That was the beginning. Since then it has appeared in many publications. I have seen it on executives' desks and in church bulletins. People write to me for copies. It has appeared in a book of prayers collected by A. G. Ford. It once cooled the temper of a New York taxi driver. A disabled man wore out his copy and sent for another. May it bless you.